THE
HITCHHIKER'S GUIDE
TO THE
Soul

Keep L.O.V.E. in
your heart
Always !

EJB

The Hitchhiker's Guide to the Soul

THE HITCHHIKER'S GUIDE TO THE Soul

A collection of scenic views of volunteerism,
transcendental encounters with kindred spirits
& lessons in compassion.

ROBERT CLANCY

Mohawk Street Press
Cohoes, NY

www.guidetothesoul.com
www.spiraldesign.com

Library of Congress Cataloging-in-Publication Data
Clancy, Robert Steven
Hitchhiker's Guide to the Soul.
p.cm.

Summary: *The Hitchhiker's Guide to the Soul* is an evocative collection of
the transcendental journeys and chance spiritual encounters experienced
through a life dedicated to volunteerism and compassion for humanity.

[1. Self-Help – Inspirational 2. Memoir 3. Essays 4. Creative Nonfiction]

ISBN 978-0-9859395-0-2

For information about permission to reproduce selections from this book,
write Permissions, Mohawk Street Press, 135 Mohawk Street, Cohoes, NY
12047 or email to permissions@guidetothesoul.com.

ɑ

Cover, Layout & Design:
Leslie Searles, Spiral Design Studio, LLC
www.spiraldesign.com

The Hitchhiker's Guide to the Soul, Spiral Design Studio and the Mohawk
Street Press logo are trademarks of Spiral Design Studio, LLC.

www.guidetothesoul.com
www.spiraldesign.com

*To all the volunteers around the world.
Keep changing this planet for the better, and
always know that you've made a difference.*

You've all touched my soul!

The Hitchhiker's Guide to the Soul

Contents

∽

Acknowledgements

༺༻

The path to The Hitchhiker's Guide to the Soul was not created by pen to paper or keys typed into a screen, but by the many beautiful kind souls and kindred spirits I have met along my life's highway. Thank you for guiding me and keeping me on my main path.

My heartfelt gratitude goes out to all who helped make this book happen.

First, to my wife and life partner Lauren—you are one of the kindest hearts I have ever known.

Next, to my son Sean, you are my greatest gift and someone who keeps giving back to me each and every day.

To my dad, for being the ultimate volunteer by landing on Omaha Beach, June 6, 1944; and to my mom, who taught me the importance of community service and compassion for others.

To my entire family, thank you for sharing your love with me and the world.

To Hugh O'Brian, for dedicating your life to making true positive change in the world.

To Ken Tarler, thank you for showing me what true living through service to humanity is.

To the Blasch family, for revealing to me what true faith in God is.

To my team at Spiral Design Studio, for inspiring me every day though your incredible creativity.

To my editor, Dawn Josephson, for helping me shape and sharpen each of the stories in this book. With your guidance, I was able to create something more compelling, meaningful and powerful.

To Ron Wachenheim for being my spell-checker in life and to the Wachenheim family for allowing me to be a superhero for a day.

Finally, thank you to all of my friends and co-volunteers around the world. You've changed me in profound ways.

Foreword

In the summer of 1958, I spent nine incredible days at a medical clinic in Lambaréné, Africa where celebrated humanitarian Dr. Albert Schweitzer, along with several volunteer doctors and nurses, worked without electricity or running water as they cared for patients, many with leprosy. I spent my days assisting the volunteers in the hospital and my nights with Dr. Schweitzer discussing global peace and world politics.

During one of our discussions, Dr. Schweitzer said, "The most important thing in education is to teach young people to think for themselves. The United States must take a leadership role in this or we are a lost civilization." Before saying goodbye to me, Dr. Schweitzer took my hand in his and asked, "Hugh, what are you going to do with this?"

The time I spent with Dr. Schweitzer was pivotal in my life. This transcendental encounter—what Robert Clancy describes in this book as a *soul hitch*—elevated my essence and positioned my life in an enlightened direction.

Combined with my unforgettable visit, Dr. Schweitzer's words compelled me to form Hugh O'Brian Youth Leadership (HOBY), a foundation committed to the advancement of our global community through the development of leadership, service and innovation skills within the lives of youth and volunteers. To date, HOBY has positively impacted the lives of over a million young people, their families and their communities.

I first met Robert while attending our 1994 HOBY Volunteer Training Institute held in Tempe, Arizona. My organization has honored him three times as a national top ten volunteer HOBY Seminar Chair, and he has freely dedicated his time and service to the inspiration of youth through my organization for nearly a quarter century. Robert is one of those people to whom I tip my hat. He is a dedicated volunteer who completely embodies the spirit of service—a selfless commitment to helping others in order to make a positive difference in the world.

Like Robert, every person has the freedom to choose his or her role in the world. If given the opportunity and encouragement to recognize his or her own potential, will an individual be a taker or a giver in life? Will that person be satisfied merely to exist, or will he or she seek a meaningful purpose? Will he or she dare to dream the impossible dream? I believe all people are stewards of their own destinies for a specific purpose: to share with others, through service, a reverence for life in a spirit of love.

The Hitchhiker's Guide to the Soul is an evocative collection of the transcendental journeys and chance spiritual encounters experienced through a life dedicated to volunteerism and compassion for humanity. Use these stories as a guide to find deeper meaning in your everyday life.

What will your next encounter with a kindred spirit mean to the world? *Everything!*

Hugh O'Brian
www.hoby.org
www.hughobrian.me

Introduction

"You can only be truly different
by being yourself."

∽

There are special moments, what I have labeled *soul hitches*, that can occur unexpectedly during everyday encounters and interactions with others. In fact, we all have the ability to hitch a ride on someone's inner spirit by keeping our essence accessible to it.

So what exactly is a *soul hitch*? It's any interaction—large or small—that changes how you view yourself, an event, or the world. It could come from a chance run-in with a stranger, from an intimate conversation with a family member, or from a breakthrough moment with friends. It could even come from a simple observation of others in everyday life, such as watching a nurse interact with a patient or a teen help an elderly person. It's something where you encounter somebody else's persona and it alters something in your thoughts that day.

Think of it as literally hitching a ride on the highway. But in this case, you hitch a ride on someone else's soul and are changed forever because a piece of the other person stays with you and resonates with your spirit.

The Ride of a Lifetime

We are all driving down life's highway, en route to our life's purpose. And we all have opportunities to exit our highway. Often, though, those exits take us off our enlightened path and into despair. In fact, I've seen some people who have taken those exits, and they never return. I believe the *soul hitches* we encounter are life's little reminders that we're driving too fast, that we need to see things differently, or that we're not doing what our soul wants us to be doing. They're there to prevent us from exiting—to revitalize our soul and give us the strength and wherewithal to keep going.

That's why I'm sharing my stories with you. I want others to realize that there are no coincidences or strange occurrences in life. The events and people you meet along your highway are messages—life lessons—to help you along your journey. You, like everyone else, are experiencing *soul hitches* on a regular basis. The key is to recognize when they are happening so you can internalize the message and use it in your life.

Give and Receive

But having life altering experiences is only half the reason for this book. In these pages, you'll see many references to volunteering—stories about my experiences as a volunteer and with leading and shaping other volunteers. That's because I believe that the more you reach out and help others, the more you'll be guided on your highway naturally.

Before we get too far, let me clarify what I mean by volunteering. When most people hear the word "volunteer," they automatically think about building houses for Habitat for Humanity, answering phones for a Muscular Dystrophy Association telethon, or canvassing the community to raise money for the American Heart Association. Those are all wonderful (and encouraged) ways to volunteer.

But volunteering goes even further. It's also about helping the elderly man across the street mow his yard, mentoring the children of the single mom next door, or even working to reunite the lost dog you found with its loving and worried owner.

Volunteering is anything you do to reach out to help another person!

Why is this important? Because our community—*your community*—is important. I've always believed that everyone should put back in the community three times what they take out. Volunteering is one way to do that.

Additionally, over the last ten to twenty years, I've witnessed many people building their wealth and material possessions—a bigger house, a better car, a fatter retirement account. Don't get me wrong…those things are important, and I strive for them too. But what happens after that? Too many people claim to feel empty—that something is missing from their lives—even though they have all the "stuff" they've worked so hard for.

What's often missing in their life is that sense of compassion, of personal growth, of spiritual renewal that you get when you give of yourself to others.

Why I Wrote This Book

Sharing personal stories with others can be intimidating. But I know that doing so is important to spread my message. When I look back over my life and assess how I attained the level of success I now enjoy, I can confidently say that it all came down to the compassion for others I've displayed and my volunteer efforts.

Often, when I share my stories verbally with others, they're captivated by messages. Some even have cried, not out of sadness, but because something I said touched them at a deep level. That has happened enough times that I knew I needed to compile the stories and share them with a broader audience.

In doing so, I want others to look at their own life stories. What encounters have you had that have shaped you? How have people impacted your life? If you really think back over your life, you'll see that you've already had many *soul hitches*. Perhaps someone said something to you in passing that made you rethink a situation. Or maybe a random act of kindness from a stranger shifted your mood—and your perception—in a positive way. These connections are there; you simply need to see them.

Now, I don't profess to be a spiritual guru or anything like that. I'm just a regular person like you. I've grown a small company, Spiral Design Studio, in upstate New York to be one of the largest design firms in the northeast, with such clients as Citibank, Disney, Activision, Konami, Staples, Home Depot and Sears. I've also dedicated more than 25 years of my life to various organizations, including Junior Achievement and the Hugh O'Brian Youth Leadership, to positively shape my community and feed my soul.

Throughout my business and volunteer endeavors, I've learned that immersive interactions with kindred spirits can lead to profound, life-changing events that carry you in new unimaginable directions and teach you incredible life lessons. When these extraordinary occurrences happen to you, simply rejoice in the universal magic that happens and enjoy the understanding of humanity.

Now, throw your thumb in the air and get ready to venture beyond the core of your soul!

Your Time to Shine

∽

I would love to hear about from you about your life-changing volunteer experiences and your reaction to this book. If there was a particular story that added meaning to your life, please let me know how it affected you.

Do you have a compelling story about a kindred spirit, a lesson in compassion, or a captivating view on volunteerism that has changed your life? If so, I invite you to submit your story to be considered for publication in the follow-up book *The Hitchhiker's Guide to the Soul: In the Shoes of Others.*

Please send your submissions to:

The Hitchhiker's Guide to the Soul
c/o: Spiral Design Studio
135 Mohawk Street
Cohoes, NY 12047
Fax: (518) 326.2342

For complete submission guidelines and online submissions, visit The Hitchhiker's Guide to the Soul website at:

www.guidetothesoul.com

Share on Facebook at: *www.facebook.com/guidetothesoul*

I hope you enjoy reading this book and that it inspires you to stay closer to your life's path and helps you recognize the kindred spirits who guide your soul throughout your journey.

Life AIN'T SO BAD

Pray

not for things, but for
wisdom & **courage.**

Yiddish Saying

What is the point to life? More important, what is the point to your life? I often find most people have not thought deeply about this, or worse, they believe they have failed their life's purpose.

❧

*J*like to play a little game with people, especially if they seem to be having a bad day. I start by asking, "What is the worst thing that could ever happen to you?" Most people offer very quick responses. Others ponder for a few minutes before revealing their unimaginable horrors.

I've heard it all—everything from being a quadriplegic to becoming suddenly blind, from losing loved ones in a terrible accident to life in prison without the option for parole, and, of course, the big D: Death. I have even received some humorous responses such as, "Increasing my taxes."

I usually chuckle and say, "Death and taxes are the two things that are not only guaranteed to happen to you, but also dreaded by just about everyone."

Admittedly, their responses are classified more as fears rather than inauspicious fates, and that is the point of this exercise.

Now for the fun part. After they reveal their deepest fears, I turn to them with a large grin and say, "That does sound pretty bad. But I've put a lot of thought into this and I actually *know* the worst thing that could ever happen to you."

At this point I have their full attention, and they urge me to disclose this most horrid nightmare. "Well, what is it?" they prod in desperation.

I pause for dramatic effect and very slowly say, "The worst

thing that could ever happen to you… is losing your ability to help another person…" I pause for an additional long moment to allow this to soak in and then add, "but this will never happen to you."

By now the person usually has a somewhat bewildered expression, so I continue to explain, "Yes, you could have some tragic accident, become blind, or fall deathly ill, but even in those seemingly terrible states you will never lose your ability to extend your hand to help another. I acknowledge the difficulty, but if you work past that, your entire soul will take on profound renewed meaning. The incredible life of fortitude lived by Helen Keller is evidence enough of that."

With this, some of the initial confusion leaves their face, so I press on. "Even in death, you can continue to have a positive impact on others through your inspirational actions. Incredible legacies can last long after you are gone. Just think about the wonderful journeys of love and inspiration outstanding individuals such as Dr. Albert Schweitzer, Rachel Scott, Mother Teresa or Anne Frank left us."

Finally, I leave them with one last thought, "Did you know you have already accomplished this task by just being you? Think carefully about all the people who you have already helped or made a difference to—those who have breathed a bit easier due to some small gesture on your part."

Their response is often silence combined with a dumbfounded look of awakening. Their spirit is suddenly galvanized with knowledge that there is truly nothing to fear but fear itself.

Like a caged bird suddenly set free, they are now able to soar higher than ever as they live their life in full reverence.

What legacy are you leaving?

Rest STOPS

There are persons

so radiant, so genial, so kind, so pleasure bearing,
that you instinctively **feel their presence**
that they do you good, whose coming into a room
is like the **bringing of a lamp there.**

Henry Ward Beecher

Some kindred spirits are like beacons
along your life's highway. They can guide you
back onto your main road or they help you
find an easier and often more scenic route.
Occasionally you will have split second chance
encounters that, if recognized, can have profound,
positive effects on your soul.

❧

To me, the first rule of a road trip is to make good time. In fact, getting to the target destination as fast as possible is not just a goal; it's an obsession. I make mad attempts to dodge traffic and avoid pit stops like a NASCAR driver with a peak conditioned pit crew.

What I despise the most are those pesky rest stops peppered all along the highway. I like to think of them as time-sucking potholes that, at any moment, engulf cars and bump schedules.

As we drive by rest stops I usually boast to my wife my prowess of having a steel-trap bladder. "I can go hours without stopping," I brag. Unfortunately for me, she can't.

During one of our annual three-and-a-half-hour pilgrimages to Long Island, I zoomed past one of those despised rest stop markers and triumphantly said, "I think I am on my way to a door-to-door record!"

That's when my wife anxiously proclaimed, "Honey, I have to use the facilities."

A man who has married eight times once told me, "There is nothing in this life worse than the scorn of a woman." His words echoed in my head, and there was no way I was going to argue against her essential bathroom break.

I reluctantly pulled into the rest stop. We both exited the car quickly—her because of nature's call and me because of my obsessive desire to make record time. We whisked through the parking lot and through the heavy doors of the station. Before we parted ways, I pleaded, "Sweetie, please be quick."

Eyeing the quickest route to the restrooms, I was immediately captivated by a young woman with a disability coming toward us. Aided by twin leg braces and dual aluminum arm cuff canes, she was slowly making her arduous journey toward the exit.

I was momentarily beguiled by the charming smile she bestowed upon the people feverishly swimming past her to make their hasty egress.

"Got to make time!" I reminded myself. I felt my internal race clock ticking and I snapped back to my mission. I continued into the lobby for another twenty feet, blowing off my most basic instinct to assist her. "I don't have time to go back and open the door," I told myself. After all, I was sure someone else would help her.

I turned my attention to my wife and said, "Can you please hurry so..," I cut myself off mid-sentence and quickly doubled back to open the unwieldy doors for the unassisted soul.

The woman's face contorted in disbelief, and I realized my delay in providing the chivalrous act must have seemed a bit odd to her. Frankly, I knew it did. My rose-tainted complexion was evidence enough of that.

The young woman locked on to my eyes, displayed a pearlescent smile, and said, "That is a great shirt! I love that show!" She was referring to the *Seinfeld* t-shirt I was proudly sporting. I expected a 'thank you' for opening the door, but not a compliment.

In this chance encounter, my mind raced between her fortitude and the kindness she bestowed upon me. "She took the time to acknowledge me," I thought in astonishment. "What a powerful gesture. This is simply a wonderful beam of light standing before me."

So struck by the moment, I only managed to fumble out, "Yes, me too… uh, yeah…it's a funny show."

Although I may never see that young woman again, our spirits are now bonded in the affinity of our sense of humor.

A universal love of humanity engulfed us both in that brief moment. It carried me from the slump of my mundane obsession to an incredible euphoric high.

I slowly made my way back to my wife and said, "Do I *really* need to be *anywhere* that fast? I should take it easy. Honey, go ahead and take your time."

With a perplexed expression wrapped around her gaping mouth, she questioned, "What? Are you okay?"

Displaying a delirious smile I said, "Yes, I'm fine. I am just going to sit here for a while," as I shriveled on to a bench.

She shrugged and then walked away to use the facilities. "She must think I am suffering from road hypnosis or something," I humorously thought.

As I waited, I sat and watched the people scurrying about. I knew this was an important lesson to take in. "How many of life's special treasures had I missed in my haste?" I wondered. "I really need to stop taking in life like a person running through an art gallery with their eyes closed. It's time to slide my soul back into first gear."

Ken

When I look back

at my experience of being confronted with death and ask myself what in that hour were the memories I treasured, I have little difficulty in answering. **I cared not for all of my personal success...**

What I did care about were the thoughts that I had **made a few happier**, that I had **done a few kindness**, that I had **won some love**.

Arthur Christopher Benson

Prejudging others has to be one of the worst sins
I've ever committed. Just like the old adage,
"You can't judge a book by its cover," the same
applies to one's essence at any given point in time.
You can't judge one's soul by its manifestation.
Is the person you just met having a bad day?
How many times have you bypassed someone
who may have something great to add to
your life just because you prejudged them
based on your initial feelings?

ભ

"We're going to take chapter of the year! After all, look who's in charge," Ken pontificated as his thumb and chest became one. "No one in the state organization will outdo my leadership."

With contempt, I thought, "Who does this 24-year-old punk think he is? I can't believe I am his district director. How am I going to work with someone this arrogant and cocky? Even this guy's dress code is off. We're all in suits and he waltzes in exhibiting an obvious lack of respect with his dress-down Friday attire."

My vinegar stained thoughts continued to ooze, "This guy just doesn't get it. People join this group to help others through our community service and leadership, not to flaunt their own ego. Apparently, he missed that memo."

Adding to my disdain, the women of the organization were all cooing over him. "Who's the new guy? I wonder if he's single," echoed several women as they glanced in his direction. This only fueled my anger.

"First impressions—you either don't get a second chance to make one, or the person making the judgment is categorically wrong. I know the outcome here," I reassured myself.

Several weeks later, a woman from Ken's group called me with some bad yet expected news. "There is infighting and other serious issues in our chapter," she said in a deeply concerned tone. "Ken yelled at all the board members at our last meeting. He doesn't listen to anyone. I don't want to be part of this anymore. I joined this organization to do volunteer work in our community, not to be scolded for freely giving of my valued time."

Relishing in his ineptness, I venomously thought, "It was only a matter of time for his type anyway." Fangs drawn, I firmly planted my callous labels on him.

I reassured her, "Don't worry. I will *take care of him* soon enough."

After hanging up the phone, I took some time to reflect on the situation. Sharpening my guillotine, I thought, "Here's my chance to teach this guy a leadership lesson he will never forget. I can't wait to take off his head and swat that chip off his shoulder."

Despite the fact that I wanted to put Ken in his place, I knew this was not going to be a pleasant or easy thing to do. Informing someone of their personality flaws is difficult, especially in a volunteer situation. People generally don't react well to personal criticism. But I was a leader in the organization and knew what had to be done.

A few days later, another group member approached me and said with a smirk, "You know…Ken will be attending the regional picnic."

"Great, now it seems everyone knows this clash of the titans is due to happen," I thought in disgust. I knew I had to put a stop to this showdown before it engulfed the entire organization.

With the upcoming awards convention fast approaching, I knew I had to act soon. I didn't want this black cloud hanging over me or the group anymore.

I decided to pull him aside at the picnic when no one was looking and keep the spectacle to a minimum. I would be both judge and jury, so I was confident I'd emerge the winner.

Finally, the moment arrived. Ken was standing alone. I walked over to him and said, "Hey Ken. Do you have a minute to speak with me?" I suddenly felt nervous.

With a puzzled look, Ken said, "Sure. Is something wrong?"

Attempting to hide my forewarning face, I replied, "Oh, I just need to review some things with you. It shouldn't take too long."

We walked away from the festivities and found a spot to be alone. Standing over him like a stolid general, I commanded, "Just listen and please don't say a word until I am done."

"Sure," he said hesitantly.

"Ken, your arrogance and ignorance is losing us members in this organization," I said bluntly. "I hope you are proud of your lackluster leadership. Are you just in this for yourself or are you too blinded by your own eminence?"

He sat motionless. I knew he was quickly plotting an onslaught of angered excuses. It was time to barricade my emotions.

"Well, what do you have to say for yourself?" I provoked.

In an apologetic and forgiving tone, Ken said, "Bob, I am truly sorry. I have failed at my goal to make a positive difference in my community. I know I can do better. Will you still give me a chance to do this?"

Shocked and stymied by his respectful response, I wondered how I could have misjudged his character and have been so far off the mark. I actually felt sorry for my negative thoughts toward him.

Infused by Ken's candor, I replied, "Ken, I need to apologize to you. My ego and foolishness prevented me from helping you reach your service goals. *I* need to do better, not *you*. I hope you will give me a second chance."

"It's mutual," Ken said with a smile. "Let's clean our slates and start over."

A couple of weeks later, Ken and I bumped into each other at the cocktail reception of the organization's awards convention. He looked pale.

"Are you sick?" I asked.

"Why does everyone keep asking me that?" he quickly retorted. "I feel fine!"

"Well you look like you have the flu or something," I rebutted.

Suddenly, a crimson stream trickled down and around his mouth.

"Not the dreaded public bloody nose spectacle," I said with a chuckle.

"This is the fifth nose bleed I've had this week," he said as he tried to quell the flow with his hand.

I sprang into action and grabbed some cocktail napkins. "This happens to me all the time. I've been prone to nosebleeds since I was kid," I said. "You should see your doctor. I think you can get blood vessels in your nose cauterized. I had this done and it cured my problem."

Shrugging it off, he said, "Yeah, this is getting annoying. I'll try to get an appointment next week."

With wads of tissues jammed in his nostril, Ken joked most of his way through the rest of the conference. His sense of humor was truly infectious—something I hadn't noticed or appreciated before.

One week later, devastating news spread through the organization like a fire running through a dry wheat field. "Are you sure it's brain cancer? Does he really only have six months to live?" people questioned in disbelief.

Others horrified by Ken's quick downturn exclaimed, "I can't believe they need to remove his eye. I just saw him last week and he looked so healthy. How could this be happening?"

The unwelcome news tore the fabric of my soul. "God's payback for my ego trip," I mournfully reflected. "Unless you have something good to say about someone, don't say it at all. For that matter, don't even think it," I berated my soul.

Shortly after his eye operation, Ken amazed everyone by attending our regional meeting. Proudly displaying a black eye patch and a reverence for life, he announced, "Well at least I'll be all set for Halloween. Pirates are in this year, aren't they?"

His words left the crowd awestruck. The abysmal ice was broken, and Ken's true spirit illuminated the room.

Even in the face of his most certain demise, Ken continued to give freely of himself. "Hey, I am no different than you. I am just doing my best to help someone else in need," he said, shrugging off any heroic compliments showered upon him.

While Ken's body weakened, his spirit for living through volunteerism became as stoic as an unbending oak tree. Ken started a program to inspire people to perform random acts of kindness. Leading the charge himself, he would stop and pump gas for people, carry groceries to their cars, and do hundreds of other seemingly small acts of compassion—always with a smile. When one of his "victims" would try to praise him, he would simply say, "Don't thank me; just do something nice for someone else."

The six-month death sentence came and passed quickly, and Ken continued to be unfazed by the group's attention. "Why are you all surprised I am still here?" he joked.

One day I pulled him aside and said, "Ken, you've beaten the odds! You are an inspiration and a beacon of hope. Do you know how significant this is?"

In typical Ken fashion, he laughed and said, "So what are you saying? Should I get a ticket to Vegas?"

"Seriously, Ken," I replied. "I have to thank you for showing me what true courage is. You've given me the ability to speak openly with people and to be truly accountable for my life. You are a rare gift."

Declining the compliment with a smile, he said, "I am no more special than you or anyone else. If you really think about it, we are all here on Earth for a short time. What you do with your time is the important thing. We only truly shine when we are helping someone else."

"Ah yes, the silver lining we all must seek," I replied with a smile.

For the next few months, Ken and I fervently exchanged insights on life and death.

"Do you think there is an afterlife?" Ken questioned.

"I am not sure what death holds for anyone in the same way the caterpillar doesn't know what it is like to emerge as a butterfly," I replied. "I know I will miss your physical presence Ken, but I will always be reassured that your precious spirit will await all of us on the other side."

"Bob, I have no real regrets or anger about what fate has dealt me. I just hoped to have enough time left to get married and to have children. I know you will be a great dad someday. Please raise your kids to be as good as you are. It is the best gift you can leave me," Ken said.

Ken defied the odds for nearly two years and astounded his doctors, but his departure was now fast approaching, and everyone knew it. "I can't believe he only has hours to live," a tearful member outpoured. In their desperation, members simply gathered together to share their sorrow.

Comments about Ken's courage, his life, and all of the wonderful things he taught them fell upon me like colorful leaves on a bright autumn day. It was a profoundly moving eulogy, yet the spirit involved was still alive!

My mind swirled until I finally blurted out, "Ken is not dead, you know!"

As I poorly attempted to retract my comment, I immediately saw the heavy black veil of fear gripping their eyes. Someone softly said, "I just don't think I can see him. I wouldn't even know what to say especially in his current condition."

"I can't argue...they are right," I thought.

Ken was now horribly disfigured and bedridden at our regional medical center. His head was swollen to the point that his eye-patch no longer fit, and a softball-sized tumor had emerged from his forehead.

I understood everyone's reservation about visiting him. In their hearts, they wanted to remember him healthy, having fun, and the way he was. I can't lie—I wanted this comfort too.

Falling into myself, I thought, "What would Ken do? What did he teach me?" Suddenly, I began to write down all of the beautiful things I heard others saying about him. I had a plan. It was so clear what I needed to do. I was again empowered, not by ego, but by love. The reverence for life Ken openly shared with me was fuel for my soul.

As I quickly made my way to the hospital, I knew our confrontation was to come full circle.

At the hospital, I approached the nurses' station and asked the slender woman in white where Ken's room was. With a huge smile, she quickly replied, "My good friend Ken is down the hall on the left. He's my special patient, and I have him all to myself. I am the luckiest person working here."

I smiled and said, "I see Ken is still working his magic."

"He is a truly a wonderful person. We will all miss him very much when he's gone," she quickly fired back. "He's going *home* very soon, you know. We really did the best we could for him here."

The gravity of Ken's nearing departure pulled me back to reality. "Yes," I said cautiously. "I will miss him too. Thank you for sharing that with me."

I walked down the hall and then slowly entered Ken's room. His deteriorated state shocked me. I could only bring myself to sit and look out the window. Staring blankly at the setting sun, I thought, "How fitting."

I didn't know what to say. I was suddenly on an emotional island deserted from my words. "How does one say goodbye to a friend?" I tormented myself.

Carefully, I unfolded my notes and said, "Ken, I am going to share with you the things most people never get the chance to hear about themselves."

I slowly read the uplifting words of his friends while a sorrowful stream of tears dripped from my cheeks on to the paper.

Suddenly, Ken's voice pierced the air like a comedian quashing a heckler. "Are you sure they were talking about me?" he joked, and we both erupted in laughter.

What an odd experience—to cry and laugh simultaneously with every fiber of your body. It is as if your entire being is shocked into an incredibly peaceful yet euphoric state.

Ken somehow knew humor would carry us to the next level. Yes, that was Ken's magic. Laughter and a positive attitude can be a cure for even the worst of times. Third lesson learned.

Ken then steered the conversation to a serious point. In the stillness of our emotional forest, he tearfully said, "I am absolutely astounded and truly moved that people think that much of me. My words cannot thank you enough for sharing this with me. I know how difficult this visit is for you, and I am blessed that you came here tonight."

We both cried, not out of sadness, but for human kindness. It was a wonderful exchange. Ken was absolutely glowing in the love that everyone freely gave to him. I was a humble messenger receiving one of life's greatest gifts.

Finally, the time came for us to say goodbye for the last time. As I stood by the door, Ken confidently said, "I'll see you soon, Bob!"

I turned to him and replied in a low, grievous tone, "Ken, we both know we won't see each other again, at least not in this life."

He nodded carefully and acknowledged the fact that I called his bluff.

As I started for the door again, a sharp whisper cut across my ears, "Bob!"

I turned around and was greeted by an ear-to-ear grin as Ken propped himself up and stoutly saluted me. I immediately reciprocated the honors. No words were spoken, and none needed to be. It was the last time I saw him and it is how I will proudly remember him.

A short time after Ken returned home, I learned that he peacefully succumbed to cancer surrounded by his family's love.

The day after Ken's passing, I carefully packaged up an anonymous gift containing an angel figurine, and I stealthily slipped it onto the nurses' station at the hospital. The card simply said, "For the wonderful soul who cared for my friend, Ken."

To this day, I continue to do random acts of kindness in Ken's honor.

Life

Dedicated in memory of Ken Tarler

∽

Don't give up on life, there is always love,
rely on its power like the wings on a dove.

Life deals us all lessons, good and bad,
just try to smile when you're sad.

If life becomes painful, don't be frightened,
just raise your chin up and become enlightened.

When life is hard it becomes our teacher,
teaching us love is its greatest feature.

Life makes you laugh and sometimes frown,
but you can always help another when they're down.

Life can be challenging and life can be hard,
just keep your heart open and you'll remain unscarred.

When your time is up and the sun sets on your life,
reflect on your love and not the strife.

Robert Clancy

Alex THE POOL MAN

If there is a poor man

among your brothers in any of the towns of the land that the Lord your God is giving you, **do not be hardhearted** or tightfisted toward your poor brother. There will always be poor people in the land. Therefore I command you to **be openhanded toward your brothers** and toward the poor and needy in your land.

Deuteronomy 15:7, 11

*I believe a reverence for others and
community comes from your family. The first
time I experienced compassion for others was at
age six. I can only attribute this to the gift my
parents passed on to me. What legacy are you
passing on to your children?*

৩৬

When I was six years old, I got to take my first airplane trip. It was more exciting than being Superman. My family and I were on our way to Jamaica for our summer vacation. I had no idea where Jamaica was or what to expect when I got there. I just knew I was going to be above the cotton-shaped clouds in a winged chariot, and that was enough.

On the flight, stewardesses dressed in exotic island garb showered my brother and me with airline fanfare. "Now you're a airline captain too," the flight attendant said as I proudly pinned the gold pilot's wings to my chest for all to see. I spent most of the flight with my nose pressed to the glass window imagining myself walking on the cotton pillows floating below.

"Touch-down!" I exclaimed as I saw the fast approaching airport.

We disembarked and entered a terminal filled with luggage toting tourists sporting colorful flowered garments, which sharply contrasted with the white-linen-clad ebony people.

"Come this way, Bobby," my mother guided as she pointed toward the terminal's exit. I stepped out into a island paradise garnished with a cobalt blue sky, palm trees, sweet ocean air, and whitewashed stucco buildings.

My dad flagged down a taxi and the smiling driver quickly loaded our bags in the trunk. "Welcome to Jamaica, man!" the driver said in a strong Jamaican accent. "Is this your first time visiting here?"

I leaped up and exclaimed, "Mister, this is my first time any-where!"

Erupting with deep laughter, the man said, "Well, then, you are in for a surprise, my friend. I know you will love my beautiful island." Motioning to the rest of my family, he said, "Every-body in the car. It's time for you to get your vacation started."

With my nose pressed against the car window, I began to drink in the exotic landscape.

"I am going to take you on the scenic route," the driver said as he maneuvered the car along the bustling streets.

The smell of the salty sea air and the sounds of kettle drum mu-sic permeated the taxi as we were shuttled to our destination.

"What kind of tree is that?" I asked in amazement. "Are those bananas hanging on it? Look! Up in that tree are a bunch of yellow birds like they have in the pet store," I said pointing to the unusual flock.

Before long, we arrived at the cottage resort that would be our new home for the next ten days. As our bags hit the floor, my brother and I ran down to the sandy oasis.

"Ahhh spiders!" I shouted as I moved a rock on the beach.

My brother laughed and said, "Those are crabs, not spiders. They won't hurt you."

I knew then that *all* the rules had changed. This was no ordinary place.

Later that day, a shuffle board court adjacent to the pool grabbed my attention. As I wandered toward the court, I bumped into one of the resort staff members.

"I am Alex, the pool man," he announced as his finger ran across the red POOL MAN letters stenciled on his white shirt. "I live up on the mountain. Who might you be, my little friend and where might you be from?"

"My name is Bobby, and this is my first time in *Janayka*," I said proudly. "And I'm from New York."

Alex bellowed out a hardy laugh and said, "Well, my friend, I'll be here to look after you then, won't I?"

The following day, I sat on the edge of the pool while Alex skimmed the leaves off the water's surface.

"Why are you not swimming, my little friend?" Alex prodded.

"I don't know how to and I'm scared of the water," I replied with trepidation.

"Well, I have to tell you, I am an expert diver. I swim to the bottom of the ocean almost every day to find treasure. There is no need to fear the water," he confidently coached.

"Really?" I exclaimed. "You can teach me how to swim *and* you've been to the bottom of the ocean? What kind of treasure did you find?"

Alex stopped skimming and sat next to me. "I will tell you all about my treasures while I teach you how to swim," he said.

"This is an important skill you must have."

While coaching me, Alex shared that he skin-dived deep into the ocean to retrieve exotic shells and coral treasures. "I sell them to all the tourists to help my village," he said. "Sometimes I have to risk my own life so that my family can survive. If you follow what I teach you, you will be a strong swimmer just like me."

The next morning I saw Alex on the beach carrying a piece of white coral and a weathered diving mask.

"Alex! Alex!" I shouted as I ran toward him.

By the enthusiasm oozing from my face, Alex knew immediately that I had sprouted my fins. He was beaming with approval. "Congratulations, little man. I knew you could do it," he said in a kind, soothing tone. "You earned a reward. Today, I will show you my secret treasure trove."

"Wow!" I exclaimed, "When can we go?"

"Right after lunch," he quickly responded. "You're gonna need a full belly for this journey."

I could hardly wait!

After lunch I met Alex back at the beach. As we walked in the surf, Alex told me about his village in the mountains and how much he cared for his family. "They are everything to me and I am rich because of them," he said. "Sometimes I must risk my own life for them by diving deep into the ocean. That's where the precious shells and pearls can be found, and I am greatly rewarded for them."

Suddenly, I saw a beautiful pearlescent balloon floating in the water, and I ran toward it. Just before I reached the purple orb, Alex, reacting like a cheetah grabbing its prey, scooped me up in his arms and tossed me onto the sand.

Clearing my eyes, I watched the ballooned object wrap around Alex's leg, which prevented it from reaching me. After jabbing the balloon with a stick and tossing it into the palm-tree lined woods, Alex kneeled down next to me. In a somber tone he asked, "Are you okay, little man? You are very lucky. *That* was not a balloon. *That* was a Portuguese Man-of-War, and they are very deadly. If that balloon touched you, you would be no more. The doctors are too far away to stop its poison."

Just then I noticed red burn marks on Alex's leg. With tears welling up in my eyes, I asked, "Did it get you? Are you going to die?"

"Don't worry, little man. I am fine. I have built up resistance to those terrible creatures," he said. He then showed me numerous other scars he attained from his diving ordeals.

Nodding my head slowly, I said, "Thank you for saving me. Your family must love you very much because you are very brave."

After a long trek down the barren beach, we reached a small hidden jungle path that guided us to Alex's secret treasure trove. Alex handed me a large empty soda bottle to collect small shells and a plastic bag for coral and conch shells and said, "Take whatever you can carry. My treasure is now your treasure."

I filled my cargo hold to the brim with pearlescent wonders and returned to my family to share the Caribbean booty I acquired.

"Wow! Where did you get all of these?" my brother yelled as I spilled the loot onto the bed.

"I can't tell you. It's a secret between me and Alex the Pool Man. He made me promise not to tell anyone," I said with conviction.

"Awww, come on," he pleaded.

Just then my mother poked her head into the room to see what the commotion was. "Those are very beautiful shells. You are a lucky boy and you have a good friend there in Alex," she said.

"Can I please visit Alex's village," I asked. "Alex told me all about it today, and I want him to take me there."

"We'll see what we can do," my mother replied. "Your dad and I have to check with Alex and the resort people first."

The next day the arrangements were secured and I was on my way with Alex to visit his village.

"I am so happy you will meet my family, little man," Alex said with a smile that beamed from ear-to-ear. "This will be a very special time for you—a very special time. Everyone in my village is waiting to greet you. I have told them all about you. They've been preparing for your arrival all morning."

After a thirty-minute drive we reached the gate to Alex's village. He stopped his car next to a large splendorous tree. "That is one of our trees of life," he said, pointing through his front windshield. "It bears much fruit to keep our village healthy."

I opened the car door and jumped out into the alien landscape, ready for my adventure. The first thing I spied was an elderly woman holding a small trowel that glistened in the sunlight. She was rebuilding mud steps attached to a small thatch roofed hut.

Bewildered at the sight, I asked Alex, "Why is your grandma making steps? Where I come from, workmen do that."

Alex chuckled. In his soothing Jamaican accent said, "Here, we *all* help build our community. Everyone is *equal*, and we all share *equally*."

I did a quick survey of the surroundings and found the entire village to be modest, with mud hut accommodations for everyone. After taking a second glance around, I asked Alex, "Are you poor people?"

With a hearty laugh and a pat on my shoulder, Alex replied, "We may not have much money, but our hearts are rich with love."

I heard laughter behind me and spun around to see a large group of children streaming out of the village. The children engulfed me in a circle and laid tropical fruit on the ground all around me. Several boys broke from the circle and climbed a nearby plush tree to harvest more fresh fruit. "More for you! More for you! Come! Come!" they yelled as they tossed avocados to me to add to the bounty at my feet.

Although the children were all dressed in worn-out clothes and didn't seem to have any toys, they struck me as the happiest group of peers I had ever met.

In a somewhat embarrassed tone, I said, "I am just like you. You don't have to do anything special for me."

Just as those words left my mouth, a villager placed a crown made of palm leaves on my head. The children then trotted a small donkey over and motioned for me to mount it. They guided the donkey and me around the village, as if I was a royal prince. It was quite a majestic experience, and the beauty of the village radiated from everywhere.

I finished my parade at the tree that first welcomed me. Alex hoisted me onto his shoulders, pointed to the valley below, and said, "Look down there to see the beauty of my island."

The view was a picture-perfect postcard that only God could create. A lush green valley wrapped in an aquamarine ocean blanket filled my eyes and my heart. That was the crown jewel in Alex's treasure, and I had this one all to myself.

☙

Forty years later, my parents and I were reminiscing about Jamaica while looking at some old pictures of our trip. When we came across a picture of Alex and me, my mom asked, "Do you remember this gentleman?"

I replied, "Yes, and I still think about his special village in the mountains. Thank you for letting him bring me there. It was an enchanted, memorable experience and something I will always think fondly of. Believe it or not, I still have some of the shells he gave me!"

My mother laughed and said, "Do you know what I will always remember?"

Perplexed, I said, "No."

"You really don't recall what you did?" she prodded.

"No, Mom...What?"

She grinned and said, "You asked us to give all of your clothes to the children in Alex's village. The only thing you returned home with were the clothes on your back."

With a gracious beam I said, "I believe I returned home with much more than that, didn't I?"

My mother nodded in affirmation. "Yes, you did…you most certainly did."

Alex the Pool Man

Jerry

To laugh often and much;
To win the respect of intelligent people
and the affection of children;
To earn the appreciation of honest critics
and endure the betrayal of false friends;
To appreciate beauty, to find the best in others;
To leave the world a bit better, whether by a healthy
child, a garden patch, or a redeemed social condition;
To know even one life has breathed easier
because you have lived.
This is to have succeeded.

Ralph Waldo Emerson

The ripples of community service are truly endless. If you've volunteered on any level, you've helped people you may never meet. You've changed lives you will never cross paths with, and you've made the world a bit better through your altruistic efforts. Community service can be anything from getting involved with a non-profit to just helping a neighbor.

☙

*M*y morning was moving along smoothly when I received my regular call from a childhood friend. "Are you able to meet for lunch today at the usual place?" he inquired.

This day was particularly stunning and I jumped at the chance to walk downtown basking in the sun. "You got it!" I replied with enthusiasm. "I'll see you at noon."

Our routine lunch spot was unfortunately deep within the bowels of the state office complex. As soon as we met, I asked, "Do you think we can take this outside today?" I was thinking of the tan I could get started on.

"No," he replied. "I have to get back to work soon and don't have enough time left in my lunch break."

Although we enjoyed our usual anecdotes about politics, sports, and volunteer work, my mind was fixated on getting back outside.

After lunch, we chatted for a few more seconds in the hallway. "You don't know what you are missing outside," I taunted, knowing full well that he wouldn't see daylight until five o'clock.

"This is one of the nicest days we've had in a dog's age."

He smiled and waved off my comments.

After we parted, I began the trek back to my office. I carefully plotted the quickest route to the surface through the underground labyrinth of marble-encased government buildings. I knew my path well, and I was anxious to see the cloudless, cobalt sky awaiting me.

Like a thief poised to steal more of this exceptional day, I was going to take my time getting back to work. Basking in golden light for a few extra precious minutes was my prize, and I couldn't wait to attain it.

I finally reached an elevator to chariot me back to the surface, and I jumped in at once. My flight suddenly took a turn for the awkward when I realized I wasn't alone in the constricted space.

An older man in a wheelchair graciously asked, "What floor do you need."

"To the ground level please," I quickly directed while I intentionally avoided eye contact with him. My head drooped into my deflated sheepish stance. I just wanted to get to the surface quickly. I hated being confined in gawky moments with someone I don't know.

Out of the corner of my eye I saw his hand moving toward me to mount a friendly attack. "Hi, I'm Jerry." he announced. Before I could respond, he continued, "You're Bob, right?"

Confused, I limply shook his hand.

He continued, "I know who you are. You volunteered for the

past three years answering the phones at the Muscular Dystrophy Association telethon. Right?"

"Yes, I did," I replied. "But the last telethon was many months ago, and I was one of over fifty volunteers. How did you remember me?"

The elevator doors sprung open for his floor. Although my floor was still a few away, I got off with him. I was an intrigued skydiver throwing caution to the wind at 20,000 feet.

Far from the rays of this perfect day, we quickly found a space to chat in the fluorescent lit marble tomb. The real light I would enjoy was sitting in front of me.

"Bob, I have something to tell you," Jerry said in a low tone. "My friend just passed away due to muscular dystrophy. He just celebrated his twenty-fourth birthday."

My expression turned to deep sadness as I thought, "I'm twenty-eight years old. What did I do with my life over the past four years—the time Jerry's friend never had? What did I waste my life on? Who could I have been nicer too? Could I have been a better person?" My racing thoughts were overwhelming.

Jerry stopped me before I had a chance to respond. "I can tell by your look that I made you feel sad, but that is not why I am telling you this," he said. "You see, my friend would have died when he was only fourteen without the medical assistance, comfort and support he received from the Muscular Dystrophy Association. He would have passed away years ago. He enjoyed ten more incredible, loving years with his family and friends."

Jerry then motioned me forward with his hand. "Bob," he said. "I have something important to share with you. Every day my friend lived beyond his expectancy he thought about and thanked the people who worked the phones in support of his life."

My eyes swelled up as I recalled why I volunteered for the telethon. Selfishly, it was for fun, free food, and a chance to be on television. I never thought about what I was doing or even if it made a difference.

Before Jerry and I parted ways, I firmly shook his hand and thanked him for sharing this wonderful story with me. I pushed the up button on the wall and turned to wait for the elevator. As Jerry rolled toward his office, the wheels of his chariot echoed against the marble slabs as they screeched to a halt.

"Bob!" he called out.

I spun toward him just as the elevator doors opened.

"If there weren't people like you around, there wouldn't be people like me around."

I simply acknowledged his praise with a devout nod, and then I turned and walked into the open elevator. His heartfelt thank you penetrated my core and permeated my soul. I was forever changed.

When I reached the surface, I hardly noticed the beautiful day. I kept the transcendental encounter I had with Jerry to myself and carried it in my heart for months, like a precious diamond.

The following spring, I was a volunteer facilitator for a group of nine high school students attending a weekend-long leadership development seminar. At our assigned group time, we grabbed a picnic table and a discussion regarding volunteerism ensued.

The students began bantering, taking various cynical positions on the subject. "I am not sure if anything I do actually helps anyone," a student blurted out. "I don't know why I've done so much volunteer work. My mom told me it looks good on a college application, so I do it," another reaffirmed. "There are so many causes out there. I can't possibly save everyone. What difference does it make? Does this even matter?"

When their cynic-filled chat died down, I made a feeble attempt to change their minds and said, "*Anything* you do to help others has tremendous positive implications, even though you may never see the results of your actions." Their underwhelming response demonstrated their skepticism.

Struggling to recover, I said, "Guys, I once felt like you do, and I completely understand your position. But something happened to me this past year that opened my eyes to the incredible gift of volunteerism."

The diamond I had been hoarding was about to radiate forth.

With their hearts and minds open, they all listened carefully as I relayed the experience I had with Jerry. With conviction I preached, "Jerry told me that without people like me around there wouldn't be people like him around. But I'm here to tell you that without people like you around there won't be *more* people like *you* around. You are incredibly kind souls who need to continue to inspire others to be like you. Don't ever give up on your volunteer efforts."

With tears in her eyes, one of the students said, "Thank you for sharing that story. I feel like I was just hit with a wave of love from all the people I have ever helped through my volunteer efforts." The other students, so overcome with emotion, could only nod in affirmation. A group hug ensued.

Their empathetic reaction was so staggering that it made me realize how special my moment with Jerry really was.

The Labor Day following the seminar, I emphatically showed up to volunteer at the telethon. This time, my soul was spilling over with drive and purpose. It was a new chapter in my life. To my surprise, six of the students from my leadership seminar group were there waiting for me.

"We want to do this with you, Bob!" they all said.

As I stood proudly with the students, Jerry suddenly appeared and wheeled himself over to our huddled group. "I see you've increased your numbers this year," he said with a grin. The students were ecstatic to meet the inspiring man from my story.

He then announced, "This is my thirtieth year volunteering at the telethon. Sadly, this will also be my last. I am retiring and moving to Florida to be closer to my children. So, Bob, I am passing the torch to you and your crew. Please carry it proudly."

Jerry smiled again and began to wheel himself away when he stopped abruptly. He spun around and said, "That day we had in the elevator was special."

"Yes," I acknowledged, "It's mutual."

I haven't seen Jerry since that day, but his love shines in all of us as bright as his smile.

Every year since Jerry's retirement, students contributing at our regional Muscular Dystrophy Association telethon have grown by leaps and bounds. Many give up their summer vacations to volunteer at Muscular Dystrophy Association camps, and they've held numerous fundraisers to support the organization.

The students have raised over a half-of-a-million dollars for the cause since then, and countless lives have been touched through their efforts.

All of this blossomed from the simple seed Jerry planted on an elevator ride I will never forget.

Jerry

VOLUNTEERING

Never doubt
that a small group of thoughtful and
concerned citizens can change the world.
Indeed it is the only thing that ever has.

Margaret Mead

*You may never get to know the people you've helped
through your volunteer efforts or how many people
you've touched. You may never fully know the love
you've bestowed in their hearts through your kindness
You may never know how much you mean to them,
even if your contribution was a small one. You may
never get the chance to hear all of the praise people
have for you. Just know that you've created a positive
ripple in the universe and that ripple is endless.*

෴

"In every community, there is work to be done.
In every nation, there are wounds to heal.
In every heart, there is the power to do it."
Marianne Williamson

"Have patience with all things but first with yourself.
Never confuse your mistakes with your value as a human
being. You're a perfectly valuable, creative, worthwhile person
simply because you exist. And no amount of triumphs or
tribulations can ever change that. Unconditional
self-acceptance is the core of a peaceful mind."
St. Francis de Sales

"May you remember that though the roads we take can
sometimes be difficult, those are often the ones that
lead to the most beautiful views."
Douglas Pagels

"The ultimate expression of generosity is not in giving of what you have, but in giving of who you are."
Johnnetta B. Cole

"Volunteers are not paid—not because they are worthless, but because they are priceless."
Unknown

"The heart of a volunteer is not measured in size, but by the depth of the commitment to make a difference in the lives of others."
DeAnn Hollis

"The best way to find yourself is to lose yourself in the service of others."
Ghandi

"I don't know what your destiny will be, but one thing I do know: the only ones among you who will be really happy are those who have sought and found how to serve."
Dr. Albert Schweitzer

ROAD
BLOCKS

We
**don't need to
change ourselves
to be kinder.**
We need change only
what we say to ourselves.
The kindest among us are those
who act in spite of the fearful and
mean-spirited voices all of us hear.

Gavin Whitsett

*Often, we encounter road blocks on our journeys
or inadvertently create them for others. These
obstructions jamming our highway of life are
built from years of negative reinforcement—
the infamous, "No." Some studies cite that
the average child hears "No" barked at them
hundreds of times each day. Due to years of
having our psyches downtrodden, we often can't
find the detour to raise our spirit. If someone
takes the time to show us this beneficial path,
our lives—and our spirits—can be renewed.*

❧

I was elected to be chairperson of a weekend-long seminar designed to help high school sophomores empower themselves to achieve their highest potential. The program can only be described as a fireworks display that is inspiring, educational, enthusiastic, motivating, and transforming. I know that the message works and resonates with the students, which is why I have dedicated almost a quarter century of my life to supporting it.

Leading up to the seminar, I received a phone call from a school guidance counselor. "Our student representative has been selected, and I am calling you to see if there will be a problem with sending her," she said in a concerned tone. I quickly told her that there was no cost for the student to attend.

The guidance counselor continued, "You don't understand. The young lady we would like to send has cerebral palsy. Her motor skills are severely impaired and she requires a wheelchair. Although she is unable to speak and write clearly, she can communicate by typing on a laptop we would provide her."

I then asked her my three standard questions, "Does this student demonstrate the most leadership potential in your school? Is she in tenth grade? Has she done exceptional volunteer work?"

"Yes, yes, and yes!" the guidance counselor said.

"Well, then, I don't see a problem. She meets all the requirements to attend," I said, putting her fears at ease.

A great sigh of relief bellowed from the woman as she thanked me profusely. "I think this program will be a great catalyst for her. I called you to confirm because she has been turned away from all the other programs we've tried to place her into," she said. The warmth of her response made me feel honored to provide this opportunity for her.

The seminar's opening day quickly arrived and all the students were streaming into the check-in area toting sleeping bags, pillows, and doting parents. For many of them, this was their first time away from home, and the fear of the unknown weighed heavily on their psyches. That is, for all but one.

Off to the side of the registration tables, a petite girl with mousy brown hair sat patiently in a wheelchair. The screen of her laptop illuminated her demure facial features as she tilted the device toward the school staff member she had in tow. Her uncontrolled, writhing hand directed her companion to move her to the check-in table.

I immediately sped over to the table to introduce myself. With a diminutive smile and a sparkle in her eyes, she simply mouthed the words, "Thank you." I openly welcomed her and went on to explain, "The only thing I ask of you is to be yourself and enjoy the weekend. There are no walls here unless you bring your own." I continued with a challenge, "Are you ready to succeed?" She acknowledged my charge with an accepting nod.

Throughout the weekend I peeked in on her and her group. The other students openly accepted her, and she became somewhat of a celebrity among her peers. Her shy smile slowly transformed into unrestrained laughter.

I learned how incredibly bright she was through the well-informed queries she fired out to various business leaders attending the seminar. Her questions were always posed by the various voices of her group using her laptop as the conduit. Although her speech was silent, her inner voice was a firecracker.

As the seminar was coming to a close, I wondered if this weekend made a difference in her life. I didn't fathom how deep her transformation ran. Like a flower in full bloom, she began to speak to the whole seminar.

Starting quietly, she began to talk about her friends back home, "When I try to speak, my friends will step in to correct and clarify what I am saying. I know they are trying to be nice, but here, my friends allow me to be me, flaws and all." As if an oppressive weight lifted, she then said, "I want to be a teacher when I grow up."

The room erupted in cheers of support.

"Sadly, my mom constantly questions my silly dream. She assures me that my disability makes my frivolous quest impossible," she tearfully conveyed to the captivated audience. "I know now my mom is wrong—I can do this!"

Emotion-filled dominos toppled across the room as everyone collectively realized she made this speech with her own voice.

There wasn't a dry eye in the house. It was an incredible sight to behold.

I knew then that her path to renewal was fully illuminated. It was now up to her to take the steps.

Several months after the seminar I was securely back into my old routines. Christmas Eve arrived quickly, and my mailbox was brimming with the usual colorful assortment of paper confections.

One card, garnished with a stark computer-printed address label, immediately jumped out at me. With a crumpled Scrooge face I immediately thought, "Who is *this lazy* that they couldn't hand address the card?"

I tore into the envelope to find a message of hope and peace for the New Year. Underneath the card's typeset message, in perfect penmanship were the words, "Thank you, from a future teacher."

Mother's Day

How far you go in life

depends on you being tender with the young,
compassionate with the aged,
sympathetic with the striving,
and tolerant of the weak and the strong.
**Because someday in life
you will have been all of these.**

George Washington Carver

*When you are your only witness, how are
you conducting yourself? Sharing love and
compassion for another without expecting any
praise or thanks in return is the best gift you can
bestow upon the world.*

⌒

*I*t was the day before Mother's Day and my mother had
only hours to live. Her breathing was heavy and she was
too weak to lift her hand or even speak. Lack of nourish-
ment and the cancer's attacks on her major organs were now
taking its toll. For the past two weeks, my family and I each
took shifts for the vigil by her bedside. Outside of my family,
an oxygen mask and pain medication were her only comfort—
or so I thought.

As I approached my mother's room, the door was slightly open
and I heard a woman's voice trickle out into the hallway. "Must
be my sister or my brother's wife visiting," I thought. When I
entered the room I discovered a lone nurse. My brother and
sister stepped out briefly when the nurse entered to check
Mom's vitals and change the bed linens. The nurse didn't notice me as I backed up quietly to observe.

I stood in the doorway and watched in awe as the nurse, instead of hastily doing her duty, carefully took my mom's hand
in hers, caressed her head, and spoke gently to her.

"You're doing *just* fine, Margaret," she said in a kind and soothing tone. "You're doing just fine. We're all here for you and we
all love you very much. Your children just stepped out for a
minute, but they will be back soon. They're all praying for you
and they love you very much. You should be very proud of all
of them. You did a great job as a mom. The special family you

raised is proof of that. It's almost Mother's Day, and you need to hang on for that. It's *your* special day."

As the nurse finished, I cleared my throat so she would know I was there.

"How is she doing?" I asked.

"She's doing fine, and she is as comfortable as possible given her condition," she replied.

"I know," I quickly responded with a smile. "She has people like you here taking care of her. I was in the doorway for the past several minutes. I heard what you said and saw the kindness in your heart. Thank you for the love and compassion you've given my mom."

The nurse chuckled and said, "And I thought only *God* was watching me."

Love

To love

for the sake of being loved is human, but to
love for the sake of loving is angelic.

Alphonse de Lamartine

The word *love* is made up of only four letters, but have you ever really thought about what the word truly means? *Love* may be a simple label we place on things that matter to us, but *love* represents how our essence is connected to the very fabric of our universe. *Love* is the light of God that connects each of us together. We can't begin to comprehend what *love* really represents to all of humanity, thus we are left with only four simple letters to describe it.

I wrote the following words many years ago in a crude attempt to explain love in the purest sense. *Love* is an acronym in which I strive to live my life.

If you fill your heart with *love*, life will always be able to mend itself, but if you fill your soul with *love*, you will be able to mend the hearts of others.

❧

Love is made up of four essential things:

*L*eadership

*O*pportunity

*V*olunteerism

*E*nthusiasm

"The reason people find it so hard to be happy
is that they always see the past better than it was,
the present worse than it is,
and the future less resolved than it will be."
J Marcel Pagnol

"In the end, it's not going to matter
how many breaths you took,
but how many moments
took your breath away."
Shing Xiong

"Happiness is like a butterfly.
The more you chase it, the more it eludes you.
But if you turn your attention to other things,
it comes and sits softly on your shoulder."
Henry David Thoreau

Happy Birthday!!!

Spider-MAN

I think you just have to

appreciate
who you are

and hopefully they can see

what a superhero is about.

❧ *Lucy Liu* ❧

Discover your true inner superhero. Each of us contains the power to change another person by just being ourselves. All of us are kindred spirits on someone else's highway.

෴

" **I** need a huge favor," my friend Ron pleaded to me over the phone. "Please, please, please, can you do this?"

"What is it? Did something bad happen? Are you okay?"

"I know you do martial arts and...well...I am in a huge bind. The guy who was supposed to perform as Spider-Man for my son's fifth birthday party canceled at the last minute," he said disgruntled. "Jared is an immense fan of Spider-Man, and I've been building him up for weeks that he is going meet Spider-Man at his birthday party. He will be crushed when Spidy is a no-show."

Suddenly, I knew where the conversation was headed, and I winced at the thought.

"I bought a professional Spider-Man suit, and I think it will fit you like a glove! You can even keep it after the party!" he said with his best sales pitch.

"Like a glove? Great. Just what I need to be wearing—a skin-tight leotard for a public spectacle," I thought with the greatest of self-consciousness. I cringed at the visual, but couldn't turn down my good friend. "Okay," I conceded. "When and where?"

"I can't thank you enough!" he exclaimed. "The party is this

Saturday at a children's arcade. I will drop off the costume at your office tomorrow morning on my way in to work."

A public venue? I thought the party was going to be at his house. I already agreed so I had to go through with it. I reassured myself that it would be over quickly. All the while, my mind recoiled in horror.

The next evening I slowly pulled the costume from its paper shopping bag and laid it out on my living room floor. "Well, it looks like it's my size," I thought. There was only one way to find out. In the back of my mind I was hoping the garb wouldn't fit so I could get out of this predicament. "Damn! It fits perfectly," I groaned.

Like Peter Parker wrestling with his inner struggles of rejections and inadequacy, I gawked at myself in the mirror in full superherodom. "Hmmmm... maybe I can pull off this stunt," I thought. "Maybe I can become this red and blue webbed avenger. It's only for an hour. How bad can it be?"

I called my friend and told him the costume fit.

"Great!" he said, "Here are the details for Saturday. You will need to be at the front door of the arcade about fifteen minutes early and wait there. You need to park your car a couple of buildings away in the shopping center parking lot and change into character there."

Almost dropping the phone, I asked, "I can't change in the bathroom at the arcade?"

"No, Jared might see you and wonder where you went. You need to approach the building in full character doing Spidy-stuff, because the front of the arcade is all glass," he explained.

"Okay, I'll make it happen according to your plan," I surrendered.

The big day finally arrived and I packed my car with my alter identity paraphernalia. After parking in a hidden area of the shopping center, I quickly discovered that getting a superhero costume on in the backseat of a car is no easy task. "How the hell does Superman get this done in a phone booth?" I wondered as I squirmed and strained to stuff my butt into the red-webbed leotards. "Okay, I just have to get the mask on straight and I'll be ready for action."

Out I popped into public ready to take down the most sinister of family shoppers. Creeping through manicured landscapes and dodging cars, I made my way to the arcade. "I am sure I am going to be arrested or something," I thought as I darted across the sidewalk.

"Look, Mommy. It's Spider-Man!" a tiny voice blurted out.

"Caught!" I thought as I struck my best superhero pose and waved at the small fan. "Just your friendly neighborhood Spider-Man here keeping our stores safe," I announced before I started scampering faster toward the arcade.

When I finally made it, I commended myself for completing this amazing feat. After a couple of minutes, the door swung open and out popped my friend. "Home free," or so I thought.

"It will be about ten to fifteen minutes or so before they'll be ready for you," he said. "Can you wait off to the side?"

"Ten or fifteen minutes? That's like an eternity!" I thought as my Spidy-senses tingled. "Sure," I relinquished.

A woman toting two small children approached the arcade and

said, "Look guys. It's Spider-Man." As I waved at them, the little boy recoiled in horror behind the woman's legs and the little girl started crying. "It's okay, honey. He won't hurt you." The woman comforted her daughter as she quickly shuttled her through the door and motioned for the boy to run to her.

"Gee, I hope they weren't going to Jared's party or this will be a complete failure," I thought.

Just then, the door swung open and the sounds of the Spider-Man theme song rolled out onto the sidewalk. "You're on!" announced my friend.

Like a nervous rock star heading down a hallway to jump onto stage, I made my way through the arcade doing Spider-Man poses and antics to a roomful of cheering parents and kids. I jumped into the middle of the swarming pint-sized fans and they all screamed, "Spider-Man!"

"Can you shoot your webs out?" one yelled. "Were you just fighting the Green Goblin?" another questioned.

In my newly discovered superhero voice, I announced, "I just received a special transmission from the alliance headquarters that it's Jared's birthday party, and the only present he wanted was to see me. Luckily, I am able to take a short break from crime fighting to fulfill his special request. What do you think of that?"

"Yay!" the screams responded.

For the next forty-five minutes, I did martial arts tricks, answered all of their deepest Spider-Man questions, and lived as a superhero. While kneeling down, I was engulfed with hugs as if I were a giant teddy bear. It was a truly uplifting experience, freeing me from my previous reservations.

Suddenly one of the kids yelled out, "I know who you are!"

"Oh no," I thought. "My cover is blown!"

The child then wrapped his arms around my neck and whispered in my ear, "You're *Peter Parker*, but I won't tell *anyone*."

"I really am Spider-Man to these kids," I thought as I gathered them all around me.

With their eyes locked on to me, I dispensed the best superhero advice I could think of: "Make sure you hug your parents every day. They love and care for you very much. The best way to say you are sorry is with a hug and smile. Love is the most powerful word in the world. Make sure you use it every day," I said as I pointed to my heart. "Spider-Man can do some special things, but your *parents* are the real superheroes. They all made all of you *super* special."

I entered the arcade an uncomfortable mortal and departed as a changed man. I journeyed back to my car exuding full superhero showmanship. I waved at passing cars, stopped for pictures in the street, and hugged people all the way to my four-wheeled phone booth.

I quickly changed into my average Joe clothes and returned to the arcade expecting to be anonymous me. Instead, I was greeted as a hero for the second time. But this time, it was the parents who showered revelry on me.

"That is one of the greatest things I have ever witnessed in my life. Thank you so much!" one parent said as he patted me on the back. "I just have to hug you!" another cheered as her arms wrapped around me. "You are truly a special man."

I nodded my head with complete humility and said, "Thank you for sharing your precious gifts with me. Your kids are truly wonderful little people. I guess we all have a superhero living inside of us. We just need a forum to release it. I am blessed and changed from this experience."

Be a superhero! You don't need the fancy costume either!

a gift from
a friend

Friends

COURAGE

We believe

in ordinary acts of bravery,
in the courage that drives
one person to
stand up for another.

Veronica Roth, Divergent

*Children, especially your own, are always
watching and learning from you. You are a role
model to them in every interaction you have in
their presence. How you behave, good or bad,
is a seed planted on their psyche. What is the
bounty you are you reaping in your life?*

༄

"Hi, I don't think we've met, but I wanted to call you to thank you and your son. He told you what he did, didn't he?" the woman inquired.

"Not sure," I replied, trying to think of a missed conversation detail after I picked my son up from school.

"If all third grade children were like your son, our schools would all be better places," she continued.

Intrigued, I asked, "What did he do?"

"I am surprised he didn't tell you. He's such a kind soul," she quickly responded. "My son has been bullied by another boy at the school for some time now. Because of this, he doesn't even want to go to school anymore. Today at the after school program, the boy pushed my son down, and your son stepped in, protected him, and told the bully, 'Stop what you are doing or you will have to deal with me! What you are doing is wrong!' That was enough to stop the bully in his tracks. Not only that, but my son feels much better about himself now and he is looking forward to going to school—something I have tried in vain to make happen since this ugliness started."

"I had no idea," I said with shock. "Sean never said a word about this when I picked him up today."

"You should be very proud of your son. He is truly a hero," she said in a loving tone. "I wish there were more boys like your son. Sean is a great role model and you should be proud of him."

"Thank you for sharing this with me," I said. "Sean is a somewhat shy kid, so I am very surprised by his actions."

After the phone call, I sat my son down and asked him, "Why didn't you tell me about the situation with the bully at school?"

He simply shrugged his shoulders and replied, "I did what you taught me to do...stand up for someone and stop bad things from happening to them. I didn't think I needed to say anything to you, because it's just something I try to do every day."

I just shook his hand and said, "You're absolutely right."

OPEN *Hearts* AND *Helping* HANDS

With open hearts and helping hands,
volunteers serve all across our lands.
Paid with love and gleaming smiles,
filled with empathy that spans the miles.

They give of their time, a special gift,
sometimes from dawn through the late night shift.
The work may be easy and often it's hard,
but only true leaders lead the charge.

Laughs and tears are what they've all shared,
everyone they've helped knew they cared.
With hearts as wide as the ocean is deep,
volunteers carry love which they sow and reap.

Without them compassion would wilt and die,
you will always find them with hope in their eyes.
Get involved so their numbers will double,
because they will certainly help you when you are in trouble.

They were taught to serve by their fathers and mothers,
to make a difference in the lives of others.
So open your heart and lend a hand,
and you too may end up in the promised land.

Robert Clancy

Beauty

The best and most beautiful thing in life
cannot be seen, not touched, but are
felt in the heart.

Helen Keller

*Acknowledging inner beauty and having the
capacity for forgiveness are two of the greatest
tools you can use to tune your soul.
It takes a good person to say they are sorry.
It takes a great person to forgive another.
True forgiveness is true inner beauty.*

❧

"*L*aVern, you just sit back and relax while I take care of the rest," my mother said as her voice echoed up from her make-shift, basement beauty shop. "You are going to look gorgeous for your daughter's wedding."

"That's why I come to you Marge," Mrs. Blasch replied. "You always make me feel good about myself and that's your gift. Thank you so much for fitting me in today and at the last minute to boot. Donna, my oldest daughter, is heading down the aisle—it gives me goose bumps. I still can't believe the wedding rehearsal is tonight. I hope it warms up a bit out there. November weddings can be challenging, but these two love birds just can't wait."

"My girls are shooting up so fast. Can you believe Mary Carol is fourteen and Sheila is already heading off to college," she continued. "Boy, do I have my work cut out for me."

"I know how you feel, LaVern," my mother chuckled as she spun the chair back around so Mrs. Blasch could see herself in the mirror.

"All done! What do you think?" my mother inquired, wearing her infectious smile.

"Marge, I don't know what I would do without you," Mrs.

Blasch said. "How much do I owe you?"

"Your smile is payment enough," my mother replied. "It's the best reward you can give me and please don't kibitz with me over the money."

"Thank you, Marge. You are a wonderful soul and a great neighbor," Mrs. Blasch said as she hugged my mother. "Oh, look at the time. I've gotta get back to my house or they will start wondering what happened to me."

As Mrs. Blasch passed me on our basement stairs, she patted me on the head and said, "Bobby, you have a good mom there. You're ten years old now, right?"

"Yep," I fired back. "I turned ten back in April."

"You're more than halfway to eleven already?" she exclaimed in disbelief. "Oh boy. You kids really are growing up too fast," she said shaking her head as she buttoned up her coat. "Can you show me out?"

"Sure," I said as I ran to open our garage door.

I watched her stroll down our driveway radiating in her uplifted spirit. Little did I know it would be the last time I saw her.

"Bobby! Wake up!" my brother shouted as he shook me. "There was a terrible accident last night and the Blasch family was hurt bad. On the way back from the wedding rehearsal, their station wagon was rear-ended by some drunk driver and it exploded."

In dismay, I bounced out my bed and asked, "Is everyone going to be all right? What about the wedding?"

"Donna and her fiancé were in a different car and they weren't hurt. But there is probably no way the wedding can happen right now. They will have to reschedule it. There are more important things they need to deal with now."

"What about everyone else?" I asked as my heart sank.

"Mrs. Blasch died in the accident," he said slowly as his voice lowered to a somber tone and tears welled up in his eyes.

"But I just saw her yesterday and she was so happy. That can't be true. Is it?" I cried, knowing the inevitable response.

"Yeah, it's true," he continued. "Mr. Blasch, Sheila, and Mary Carol were all burned pretty bad, but they are alive. I think gas from the car spilled on them and caught fire. I heard Bernie was thrown from the car and cleared the flames. They're all in the hospital now. Luckily, the rest of the family was in a different car."

"What can we do?" I said, feeling helpless.

"Pray for them," he said. "It's the only thing we can do right now."

For weeks the entire neighborhood bonded together in prayer and support as details of the Blasch family's recovery trickled in.

Several months passed. Then, on a cold winter day, my brother excitedly burst into my room. "I just found out that Mary Carol will be coming home tomorrow, but Sheila will be in the burn unit for at least another few months," my brother said as concern washed over his voice. "Before you see her, I want you to know what happened to her and Sheila because I think you are old enough to handle it. Mary Carol was burned on the side of her face and neck, and she lost her hair. Sheila's entire face, head, and hands were severely burned. They won't be the same ever again."

"But Mary Carol and Sheila are both so pretty," I said in anguish. "Why did this have to happen to them? I just want them both back to the way they were. The whole neighborhood just isn't the same."

"I know how you feel, Bobby. I wish things were the back to normal too," he sorrowfully comforted. "We just need to be strong so we can love and support them. Mary Carol and Sheila are still the same people inside, even though their outsides have changed."

Just then, the magnitude of the accident's damage must have overtaken him. He clenched his fists and asked, "Do you have any idea how much anger I have at that drunk driver? Do you know what I would do to him if I ever saw him?"

The next day, my brother's rage turned to cries of joy that echoed down our stairs all the way to our den. "Hurry! Come on up, Bobby. Mary Carol is here!"

Peering from our front door, I saw a slender figure in our driveway wearing a down-filled jacket, a wool hat, and a smile. White bandages were poking out from under her hat.

"I missed you guys," Mary Carol said as she stretched out her arms for the ensuing hugs. "I am so happy to be back home!"

"Mary Carol! How are you feeling?" my brother prodded as he wrapped his arms around her. "When do you get those bandages off?"

"Oh, I'm doing fine," her ever cheerful voice rang out. "The bandages will be off soon, but I don't think my hair will ever be the same. I am very thankful to be alive. God must have some plan for me—just not sure what it is."

"How did you deal with all that time in the hospital?" my brother asked.

"I was in a medically induced coma for a couple of weeks, and I was very disoriented when they woke me up. They must have thought I was crazy when I kept saying weird stuff. After that, I was pretty much bored out of my mind most of the time," she replied, without skipping a beat.

"Once I came to my senses, I just wanted to meet and forgive the man who did this to us. Oh well, that just about sums me up," she said matter-of-factly.

"What?" my brother exclaimed. "Are you kidding me? Forgive that guy? All I thought about was knocking his head off for you."

"I appreciate that Dave, but I'm at peace with this. We all need to be at peace with this."

Stunned by her grace and clemency, we just hugged her again. Mary Carol's ever optimistic personality radiated forth, and that is her true beauty. It was the first of two gifts the Blasch sisters bestowed upon me.

Several months later, spring weather swept over our street along with some long awaited good news. "My sister is coming home this week," Mary Carol cheered as she ran up our driveway. "I think my brother Denny is going to fly the big kite too! We just need a good windy day."

"Cool-beans!" I exclaimed. "How is Sheila feeling? I really miss her."

"She's doing much better, but she's scared to see everyone. She definitely misses all of you guys," Mary Carol replied. "The kite will hopefully get her motivated to come out."

A few days later, the breeze was just right and the monster kite emerged from the Blasch's garage.

"Get the gang assembled!" Dennis yelled out as he laid the massive, red kite out on the driveway for a last minute inspection. "We're going to need all hands on deck."

My brother quickly ran off to round up the other kids from the block, while I stayed to watch the pre-flight checks.

"Denny, how big is your kite's wingspan?" I asked, marveling at the curiosity. "Five feet, at least. My dad built this monster," he responded as he placed a large wooden string-filled spool next to me.

"Whoa! That looks like a Jeep winch! That's miles of string!" I exclaimed. "I am so excited. I've always wondered if this kite could fly. It's been hanging in your garage forever."

"Well, we're just gonna have to find out if this thing still has some air miles left in it. My sisters deserve something special," he said. "They've waited too long to see this. It's only been in the air once or twice."

A crowd of kids gathered around the kite and helped transport it to its designated launch zone.

"We need four of you to hold the kite and its tail," Dennis directed. "Two more of you to man the spool and the rest can help guide the string while we run it up for launch. Let's do this!"

"Yay! There it goes!" the crowd cheered as the red beacon of hope took to the sky. "We did it!"

As the kite lifted off, I saw a slender figure walking slowly toward us. "*Sheila*," my mind raced as fear gripped me. "What do I say to her?"

My social tools to handle this situation were rudimentary at best. I had never dealt with something this tragic. Frankly, most people never do in their entire life. I wasn't sure if I could even look at her, so I took refuge in my memory of her beauty.

Just as the kite shrunk to the size of a tiny red dot in the sky, the string suddenly snapped. "Oh no!" the crowd yelled out.

"Quick, let's go get it. I think it landed in the woods!" my brother exclaimed while he rallied the mob to go on the recovery expedition.

The remaining string began to fall all around me like a spider web drifting down from the sky. "I can help wind the string back up," I yelled to the group as they all scrambled into the woods.

Sitting alone in the grass at the top of our street, I started to wind the string back onto the spool when thin legs in blue jeans appeared next to me.

"I think I can help you with that," Sheila said as she knelt down next to me.

Averting my eyes to the ground, I replied, "Okay," in a frail apprehensive voice. "I really missed you."

"It's alright to look at me," she said softly as she took my hand in hers. "It doesn't hurt anymore, and at least my temporary nose doesn't fall off now," she continued in an attempt to lighten the mood.

We sat in a moment of silence—my eyes still looking toward the ground.

"Being home again is one of the best gifts I could be given," she continued. "Life is a precious gem and I am very thankful for mine. My mom taught me faith in God above all else, and I take great comfort in that. I know you prayed for my family and me, and for that I wish to thank you with all of my heart."

With the ice broken, I slowly gazed up at her face to see her new portrait. Instead of seeing a disfigured person, I only saw a beautiful soul. Inner beauty is the endowment Sheila lavished on my life that day.

I've heard the phrase "beauty is only skin deep," but I have to revise that one to say, "True beauty is carried deep within each of our souls."

Mary Carol and Sheila's kindness, forgiveness, and compassion through their faith in God are their true beauty. They are precious gifts I will always carry with me.

The GREATEST

I am the greatest.

I said that even before I knew I was.

⤺ Muhammad Ali ⤻

*Each of us is a leader in some form or another
even if we are not in a physical leadership position.
We lead through our compassion and our acts of
kindness. Never lose sight that someone always
looks up to you.*

୧୨

*J*ust following the 1996 Olympic Games, I was given an incredible opportunity while volunteering at a benefit dinner held at The Waldorf Astoria Hotel in New York City. The main honoree for the event was Olympic Gold Medalist and legendary Heavyweight Boxing Champion Muhammad Ali, and I was selected to escort him and his wife Lonnie in and out of the packed reception.

"Our honored guests are right down there," the event director said as she pointed to the private waiting room. I straightened up my tuxedo and headed into the lounge.

"Right this way, Mr. and Mrs. Ali," I said with a bit of trepidation in my voice.

Mr. Ali motioned me forward and asked, "What's your name, sir?"

"Uh...Bob," I stumbled out.

"Bob, don't be nervous. I'm Muhammad, and I'm no different from anyone else," he said in a low scruffy whisper as his trembling hand patted me on the shoulder.

"I am pleased to meet you," I said as we shook hands.

"He struggles so much with that terrible Parkinson's disease," his wife said calmly while she smiled at me. "He may need your shoulder to use as a guide. Just keep an even pace to your walk and he'll be just fine."

The man who shouldered the world was using my shoulder to support himself. It was quite the juxtaposition and an honor.

As I led Mr. and Mrs. Ali toward the reception room, the chatter of hundreds of conversations permeated the hallway. So many voices overlapped that it was just a crescendo of white noise as I grabbed the door handle.

Mr. Ali crossed the threshold and the entire room stopped dead in a collective hush. It was as if the air was sucked out of the room all at once.

"That happens all the time," his wife said chuckling. "He's got quite a presence, don't you think?"

"Wow! That is truly incredible," I replied. "I've never witnessed anything like that in my life."

"I always have a front row seat to this and I never grow tired of it," she said in adulation. "He's truly led an incredible life. I am so blessed to be a part of it."

As I led Mr. and Mrs. Ali to their seats, the event director motioned me over and said, "Please try to keep the autograph seekers to a minimum. Mr. Ali doesn't like to be inundated with signing too many items, and we certainly don't want him hounded during his dinner. Immediately following his acceptance speech, please escort him and his wife back to the private lounge."

I affirmatively nodded and said, "I'll do my best."

As people streamed over to the head table, I stood guard and bounced them away one-by-one. "This is going to be an auto-graph-crazed, paparazzi madhouse when this event is over," I thought. "I can't believe how many people have approached him toting the event program and a pen. If I wasn't here, he probably wouldn't be able to eat at all."

When Mr. Ali finished his speech, people began to crowd up around him with their pens and program books waving. I was trapped in the middle of the swarm with him and his wife as the urgent requests rang out. "Muhammad, can you sign this for me!" "Over here, just your signature please!" "Muhammad! Muhammad! I am a big fan!" the cries blared.

"There is no way I can control this," I thought as I plotted a course for the exit.

"Right this way, Mr. and Mrs. Ali," I said as I led my party to the door with the seething mob in tow all around us.

"They look like a school of hungry fish following their prey," I thought as more people joined the crowd of gawkers.

Suddenly, Mr. Ali changed direction and started heading back into the ballroom.

"Mr. Ali, the door is this way," I guided, but he kept steady on his new course. I was totally confused. "Where are you going?" I asked as my expression turned to complete puzzlement.

It was at that moment that I spotted his target—the small girl leaning against a pillar with her head hanging down in despair. The pen in her limp her hand was pressed against Mr. Ali's pro-gram book photo. I am sure she saw the immense crowd of greedy autograph seekers and simply gave up in discouragement.

When Mr. Ali reached her, he placed his hand under her delicate chin and thoughtfully raised her head up to face him. She looked completely shocked at first, and then her face lit up in disbelief. Mr. Ali took her pen and booklet, carefully signed it, and handed it back to her. It was one of the few autographs he gave out that night.

The crowd was stopped in their tracks at this act of compassion, and they simply cleared a path for Mr. and Mrs. Ali to exit the room without any further interruptions.

As I stood behind Mr. Ali marveling at his incredible persona, I thought, "He really *is* the greatest."

Stephanie

There is one thing

one has to have: either a soul that is cheerful by nature, or a
soul made cheerful by **work**, **love**, **art**, and **knowledge**.

⊱ Friedrich Nietzsche ⊰

*Enthusiasm is a great catalyst for
remarkable changes in your life path.
Like street lights guiding you on a highway,
positive energy will direct you to new heights
you may have never dreamed of. The more
positive you are in your outlook, the more
opportunities that will unfold for you and the
more kindred spirits you will meet.*

✿

"I don't think I will get into college," Stephanie, the demure student, said while she drowned in her shyness.

"Finally she is opening up," I thought. "Maybe this peer-to-peer group dynamic is actually working."

"Have you scouted any colleges yet?" a student in the group prodded. "You should be able to get into a college if your grades are good enough."

"Your grade point average should be pretty good... or else you wouldn't be at this leadership conference," another student added.

Trying to help, I blurted out, "I graduated a few years ago. The application and selection process wasn't too bad, so..."

Stephanie interrupted and said, "Well, I'm just my high school track & field star. I am certainly not class president or valedictorian material. I am really scared." Tears started streaming from her eyes as she said, "I am just not sure about myself."

Suddenly, a spontaneous group hug engulfed her, and I saw her smile for the first time.

"We love you, Stephanie!" one of the students yelled. "We know you can do it!" another cheered. "You are part of our team and we will always be there for you." It was a beautiful moment of compassion and caring.

The next morning, the change in Stephanie was obvious to everyone. She was glowing with a renewed spirit. I sat back and watched her personality unfold like a rose in the sun.

"I am so glad you decided to come to this conference, Stephanie. You really are a wonderful person," I said in a gracious tone.

"I am glad I applied to be here too," she said. "I almost didn't and that would have been a huge mistake."

Suddenly, Stephanie jumped up from her seat and yelled, "Let's go! It's time for our group to lead one of the cheers!" Stephanie ran to the podium with her group in tow and a 300-person enthusiastic cheer ensued with Stephanie at the helm.

Sunday came quickly and the conference drew to a close. All of the energized spirits were being released back to their families and communities, and this is where the real magic begins.

At our final group meeting, I said, "This may be our last time together as a group, but this is not the end. This is your new beginning. Make something positive happen with this exceptional gift you've been given. Be outstanding, and always know you've made a difference in someone else's life—mine."

The group formed a circle and everyone placed their hands into the center. "Stephanie deserves to take the top spot," someone yelled. "Absolutely!" the group cheered as they raised their hands in adulation.

Just after the closing ceremony, I turned to find Stephanie and her mother standing behind me with outstretched arms. "My mom and I just want to give you a hug," she said. "This conference has changed my life. I hope you do this every year from now on so other kids like me get this opportunity."

Her mother chimed in while trying to hold back tears: "I am not sure what you did all weekend, but I have to tell you that my daughter has changed for the better, and I really like it."

Trying to shrug off my volunteer effort, I questioned, "But we were just having fun this weekend, right? How did this have this kind of effect on you?"

"This is the first time I felt like I could be myself," Stephanie said. "Now I know who I really am. That shy girl that came to this conference is leaving as a changed woman. I know what I am capable of now!" Tears of joy poured from her cheeks.

I was not expecting this transformational result and was stunned to have been a part of it. "You are a special person," I coached. "Don't ever forget that. I hope you apply to be a junior staff member for next year's conference."

"I will as long as you promise to come back, too!" she exclaimed as she took my hands and gave them a squeeze.

The following year I returned to serve as a group leader. As the new staff streamed into the pre-seminar orientation, I was thrilled to see Stephanie's shining smile among the crowd.

I walked up to her, hugged her, and asked her how she's been doing.

"Believe it or not, I was elected class president," she said beaming from ear-to-ear. "I also went to Washington D.C. over the summer and attended the Presidential Classroom program there. I actually met the President of the United States!"

Reflecting back on that shy girl I met a year earlier, I thought, "She wasn't kidding. She really is changed...and for the better. Her enthusiasm is absolutely infectious."

She continued, "I am here because I want to give the next group of students the experience and opportunity you gave me."

"It's mutual," I quickly replied as I pointed to my heart, "I am here because you inspire me."

The next morning, Stephanie and I watched as the new class of student leaders arrived looking like a herd of deer with their eyes in the headlights. Stephanie chuckled at the sight and asked, "Is that what I looked like last year? Wow, have my eyes been opened since then!"

Just then the cheers started to ring around the startled new students. "O-U-T...S-T-A-N-D...I-N-G, Out, Out, Outstanding!" they clapped and chanted as they motioned for the new students to stand. Enthusiasm, smiles and positive energy filled the room like a floodlight illuminating a dark void. Watching Stephanie leading the charge with her hands held high in the air, I thought, "This is what did it. This positive, accepting environment created by the volunteers. This is what helped Stephanie and the other students see their potential."

Later that day the annual sponsored Troy Kiwanis barbecue ensued, and Stephanie and I made our way to the food line. "One cheeseburger, please," I requested.

"Sure thing. Coming right up. Ketchup and mustard are at the other end of the table," the man replied as he placed a burger on my open bun.

"Thank you, sir!" I said with a wink. "Your annual support of this conference really does make a difference in our community."

"I would also like to thank you," Stephanie added. "I am one of your '*differences*'!"

The man chuckled and said, "It is our honor to be here for you. Make sure you get enough to eat. We've got plenty."

As Stephanie made her way to a shady spot near a tree, a scream rang out. "Stephanie! Stephanie! It's your mother! She's on the phone and needs to speak with you right away! You need to go to the operations room right now!" the staff person cried. Stephanie's smile dropped as quickly as her plate as she ran into the building.

I almost spilled my plate as I nervously sat under a tree behind the grills. With my appetite diminished, I wondered what this terrible news was. "This seems serious," I thought. "I hope her family is alright."

I kept my eyes trained on the door for Stephanie to emerge. It felt as though an eternity of agonizing time passed. Finally, she stepped out, but her body language foretold that she received some serious news. Her eyes were red and the tears were still visible on her face.

As I started toward her, she motioned for me to move quicker.

"What is it?" I gasped. "Is everything alright? Do you need to head home now?" I reluctantly inquired.

"I just spoke with my mom," she said as her lips quivered. "I was accepted to college!"

"That is outstanding!" I cheered. "And you thought you wouldn't get in."

"I am not done yet," she added with a new rush of happy tears flowing down her cheeks. "I was accepted to go to *Harvard*...on a *full scholarship*! I want you to be the first to know this, because I am so grateful to you. I wouldn't have this opportunity if it wasn't for this program and for you being here for me."

As she wrapped her arms around me in gratitude, I said to her, "I always knew you had this success stored in you. It just needed a window of light shown on it so it could grow and flourish."

And flourish it did!

Reflections
EXERCISE

A smile is the light
in your window that tells others that there is
a **caring**, **sharing** person inside.

— Denis Waitley

This reflections exercise helps volunteer teams or any group bond, get to know each other, and understand one another on a deeper, personal level. It will help develop a team dynamic where there is open communication among the group. Participants move past surface impressions and, in turn, create a sense of community and bonding among the group.

෯

Participants must place trust in each other and be sensitive to the feelings of everyone in the group by listening carefully to what each group member shares.

Group Leader Instructions

1 Choose a quiet space and have the entire group sit comfortably in a circle.

2 Ask everyone to close their eyes, relax, clear their thoughts, and close out the world around them. Allow one to two minutes for this step.

3 Ask the members of the group to think quietly of both a *recent meaningful experience* and a *recent happy experience* to share with the group. No talking should occur during this stage of the exercise. Allow three minutes for this step.

4 To the group, say, "While someone is speaking please remain quiet. Focus on what the other person is saying and try not to think about what you are going to say."

5 Starting with you (the Group Leader), go around the group and have each member of the group share their two (2) experiences with the team. Ask the team to keep their responses to a maximum of two to three minutes each.

6 After everyone has shared their experiences, have each member of the group share a response to someone else in the group on something that group member said that touched them.

RENEWING
Your Soul

HELLO

What can you ever really know
of other people's souls—of their **temptations**,
their **opportunities**, their **struggles**?

One soul
in the whole creation you do know:
and it is the only one whose fate
is placed in your hands.

C.S. Lewis

Don't let negative thoughts or perceived
negative opinions of you permeate your soul.
Love does conquer all, and love must first
start with love of self.

ᘯ

"They posted hurtful comments on Facebook about how I looked in my prom dress. I thought these girls were my friends," one teenager relayed to the group of her peers. "I was more shocked than I was upset, *at first,* but then those awful words got to me," she solemnly said as tears rolled down her cheeks.

"When I was in junior high, I was called names that still ring in my ears today," another teen shared. "That ridiculing still has a negative effect on me. It's hard to shake something like that when it's stabbed you to your core."

One after another, the group and I sat quietly and listened to these gut wrenching stories. "Words," I thought. "They really are a devastating weapon."

My mother once told me, "If something bad happens to you, share it with as many people as you can and they will each heal a little piece of your hurt. But if something good happens to you, hold it in as long as you can so it fills your soul up with its goodness."

"It's probably a good thing that they are sharing this hurt that has been bottled up in them," I thought. "It's the biggest step in their healing process."

After the last student shared their distressing story, I said, "I am going to tell you something that I wish I learned when I was your age. I am a bit older now and hopefully I am a bit wiser. First, I want you to know how I feel about all of you."

In a soothing tone, I continued, "I am sitting in this circle with some of the most beautiful souls I have encountered, who fail to realize how graceful and meaningful their lives are. In your young lives, you have already made a positive difference in someone's life through your volunteer work. You have touched your family and friends in profound ways that you may never know, and each of you is a special being—in fact, we all are. Never forget that."

"The only opinion that really matters is the opinion you have of yourself, and that should always be a positive one. You know who you are deep inside, and you should always believe in that person," I said confidently. "The only word that should matter to you is love. Love is the most powerful word we have in our language and it conquers all others," I said with a smile.

"I often encounter sad souls who get their tiny precious cup of positive energy drained, spilled or crushed by others. These poor people try in vain to guard their beloved cup from these negative *soul-suckers*, but their cup is too fragile to handle attacks such as critical comments, negative labels, the perceived thoughts of others, and even their own low self-esteem. I know because I was one of those people," I confided.

I finished the moment by saying, "Know now that you don't need your precious cup anymore, because you are always standing on a beach with an entire ocean of love, support and compassion right behind you. You just need to dip your toes in."

Are your feet on the beach?

Perseverance

Nothing
is impossible;
the word itself says,
"I'm possible"!

Audrey Hepburn

Large, seemingly insurmountable goals
can be overwhelming. I have often said that
if I was told everything I had to do to become
a successful entrepreneur on the first day of
my business venture, I would have given up
on the spot. I have always viewed massive
goals like the staircase in a skyscraper.

࿐

*J*f I gave you the lofty goal of climbing the stairs in a 100 story building with over 2,000 steps, you might faint at the thought.

However, if I broke the task down into smaller goals, such as, "In the next 10 minutes I would like to you climb to the third floor and then take a break on the landing there to celebrate your success. Once you have accomplished this task I will give you your next goal, and so on," then you just might succeed at this mission. The key is stringing the small goals together.

This is the power of perseverance and small wins.

"On the mountains of truth you can
never climb in vain: either you will reach a point
higher up today, or you will be training your powers
so that you will be able to climb higher tomorrow."
Friedrich Nietzsche

"In the confrontation between the stream
and the rock, the stream always wins—
not through strength but by perseverance."
H. Jackson Brown

"If I had to select one quality,
one personal characteristic,
that I regard as being most highly
correlated with success, whatever the field,
I would pick the trait of persistence.
The will to endure to the end,
to get knocked down seventy times
and get up off the floor saying,
'Here comes number seventy-one!'"
Richard M. Devos

"I learned about the strength you can get from a
close family life. I learned to keep going, even in bad times.
I learned not to despair, even when my world was
falling apart. I learned that there are no free lunches.
And I learned the value of hard work."
Lee Iacocca

"Defeat is simply a signal to press onward."
Helen Keller

"The miracle, or the power, that elevates the few is to be
found in their industry, application, and perseverance under
the promptings of a brave, determined spirit."
Mark Twain

"Patience and perseverance have a magical effect before which
difficulties disappear and obstacles vanish."
John Quincy Adams

Summits

I've learned that
**everyone wants to live
on top of the mountain,**
but all the happiness and growth occurs
while you're climbing it.

≫ *Andy Rooney* ≪

When considering true growth, I believe if you are not growing, you are dying. You should never pass up an opportunity to learn. It is the goal of every living creature to reach toward the light, whether it's the sun or a positive ideal of simply reaching your hand out to help another person. Nothing illustrates this concept better than Chris Waddell's odyssey climbing Africa's Mount Kilimanjaro.

಄

*I*n 1988, Chris Waddell, a promising young skier at Middlebury College, was left paralyzed from the waist down after a skiing accident. Determined to get back on the slopes, he began skiing on a monoski less than one year later. In two more years, Chris was named to the U.S. Disabled Ski Team.

Through sheer fortitude, Chris went on to become the most decorated male skier in Paralympics history, winning 12 medals over four games and spending 11 years on the U.S. Disabled Ski Team.

Surprisingly, this is not his legacy.

In 2008, Chris established a personal goal to change the world's perspective about disabled people by reaching the highest place he could climb. "How can they not notice me on top of a mountain?" he said, "This is how I can make a difference and connect with the people all around the world. I don't want to be alone or separated anymore. This is a universal struggle we all face in life."

Mount Kilimanjaro was focused in Chris's sights, and he set out to become the first paraplegic person to climb it unassisted.

During one of Chris's scouting visits to Africa, he met a young, stoic man named Tajiri. Tajiri was a guide on Mount Kilimanjaro before a rockslide took his leg. Chris was taken by Tajiri's story, and bought him a light prosthesis that fit well enough to climb with. Chris also encouraged Tajiri to tag-along with Chris and his team on their journey to the summit. With Chris's encouragement, Tajiri agreed.

Chris knew the prosthetic leg wouldn't be enough to get Tajiri his old job back, but he wished it would at least allow him to dream again. "I wanted to reconnect Tajiri with the mountain to give him hope through the climb. Without hope, you can't be empowered," said Chris.

On September 24, 2009, Chris began the daunting climb with a special off-road handcycle modified by his team member, Dave Penney. Dave, an experienced climber, knew Mount Kilimanjaro had one section that Chris's climbing cycle would have great difficulty in passing.

Since Chris had surprised Dave greatly during the training for the climb, Dave kept this insight to himself in the hopes Chris would find a way to overcome the obstacle. Dave also believed climbing a mountain was about making it to the top and had not defined victory as narrowly as Chris.

After 12,000 grueling feet into the 13,000-foot journey, Chris encountered a boulder field on the crater rim. After several futile attempts at overcoming it, he relented to the mountain.

Faced with failure, he knew he would need assistance to complete the climb. "I didn't just stare defeat in the face; I swallowed it whole," said Chris.

To reach the summit, Chris's team would have to carry him for

100 of the remaining 1,000 feet.

The next day, Chris's climb team ferried him over the 100 feet of obstacles. Although the helping hands covered him like a warm blanket, Chris grappled with the loss of his personal goal. Once the team reached the other side of the boulder field, Chris took Dave aside to tell him how disappointed he was.

"You knew about this didn't you?" Chris questioned, "Why didn't you tell me?"

"Chris," Dave said, "no one climbs a mountain alone."

"If I didn't need anyone, I was separate. I was alone," Chris realized. The feeling of being separate was what Chris had wanted to eliminate the whole time. With a renewed spirit, Chris went on to climb the rest of the way to the summit, unassisted, knowing that he'd had an epiphany.

At the summit, it was evident that his gift to Tajiri was far greater than just a prosthetic leg. Beaming from ear-to-ear, Tajiri said to the other guides, "You never thought you'd see me here again. Well, I'm back!"

"Tajiri was no longer a shell of a man, he was again complete," Chris thought.

Worried about how the world might perceive his feat, Chris found comfort in knowing he had already changed one person's life.

"It's not what happens to you," Chris said, reflecting on this climb's profound affect on him, "It's what you do with what happens to you. And, ultimately, how we create a community that allows all of us to live fully."

Growth involves accepting a helping hand from another. Success is about freely giving yourself to help another. We are all connected through our humanity in one way or another.

One Revolution is Chris Waddell's motto for this expedition, and now for his life. "One revolution means so many things to me," he said. "One revolution of the handcycle, one revolution of the earth, one lifetime, one moment, one chance to make a difference."

Chris draws from his personal experience to motivate and inspire others. He has touched the lives of more than 100,000 children through programs that address negative labels, and his foundation helps change the way that the world views people with disabilities by demonstrating the common experience of challenge.

How are you changing the world?

෮

To learn more about Chris Waddell and *One Revolution*, the documentary of his incredible climb, visit www.one-revolution.org.

Smiles

All people smile
in the same language.

Proverb

*Community service can be as
simple as just smiling at someone.
A smile is a powerful tool people all carry
with themselves every day, but more often
than not, they don't take the initiative to use it.
Smiles can close a business deal, warm someone's
heart, or start you on the road to recovery after
an illness. Smiles are the only contagion we need
to spread from person to person.*

ॐ

"**W**ait here. I will only be a couple of minutes. You are eight years old now so I'm trusting you to behave yourself," my dad said as he closed the car door.

As my dad disappeared into the airport, a large black limousine slinked into a parking spot just across the lot from me. I carefully watched as the door of the limo slowly opened. To my dismay, horror film actor Vincent Price emerged from the wheeled coffin, wearing a scowl as ominous as his black suit.

I was terrified because this was the man who scared the living daylights out of me. My brother tormented me every Saturday night by turning on *Chiller Theater*, a weekly television program that showcased classic horror movies. Through this show, I watched—or rather, endured—Price's horror film classics such as *House of Wax*, *The Pit and the Pendulum*, *The Haunted Palace* and *Scream and Scream Again*. After trembling through these movies, I had to be carried to bed due to my gripping, movie-induced fear of the dark.

Unfortunately for me, Mr. Price glanced at my dad's car and noticed me staring at him. "Oh no!" I thought as my jaw dropped faster than a stake driven through a vampire's heart. "He didn't see me. Did he?"

Walking like a zombie with his arms dangling at his side, Mr. Price scuffed his way sluggishly toward my dad's car. "He's gonna get me!" I cowered. Cold fear draped across my face. My body coiled up into the fetal position on the car seat.

He finally reached my dad's car and slowly turned toward me with a gaunt blank stare in his eyes. Slowly, he bent down and placed his menacing face directly in my window and pointed his long, boney index finger at me. By now I couldn't even breathe. My heart was practically pounding out of my chest. I sheepishly raised my eyes up toward his face. His expression of doom loomed over me like a somber undertaker ready to close a coffin.

Just then, his face lit up with a huge ear-to-ear gregarious smile, and we both burst out laughing. He waved his hand at me in a friendly manner and laughed his way into the airport.

From that day on, I never had a fear of the dark again. Smiles *can* change lives.

Death

RIP

Death is nothing else

but going home to God,
the bond of love will be unbroken
for all eternity.

Mother Teresa

Death is never an end, but rather a chance for something new to begin. While most people think of death in the literal sense, it can also have a figurative meaning. For example, death can be a complete change in your life direction, such as a move across the country or a separation from everything familiar to you. Regardless, death should not be feared because it always contains a silver lining. You just have to look for it. The darkest of nights can always inspire a brightly lit dawn.

ॐ

"Death is not the end.
Death can never be the end.
Death is the road. Life is the traveler.
The Soul is the Guide."
Sri Chinmoy

"I believe there are two sides to the
phenomenon known as death,
this side where we live, and the other side where
we shall continue to live.
Eternity does not start with death.
We are in eternity now."
Norman Vincent Peale

"Seeing death as the end of life
is like seeing the horizon as the end of the ocean."
David Searls

"There is no death! What seems so is transition;
this life of mortal breath
is but a suburb of the life elysian,
whose portal we call Death."
    Henry W. Longfellow

"Death is not the greatest loss in life.
The greatest loss is what dies inside us while we live."
    Norman Cousins

"When you were born, you cried and the world rejoiced.
Live your life in a manner
so that when you dies the world cries and you rejoice."
    Native American Proverb

"What we have done for ourselves alone dies with us;
what we have done for others and
the world remains immoratal."
    Albert Pike

"Normally we do not like to think about death.
We would rather think about life.
Why reflect on death?
When you start preparing for death you soon realize
that you must look into your life now...
and come to face the truth of your self.
Death is like a mirror in which
the true meaning of life is reflected."
    Sogyal Rinpoche

Halos AND PITCHFORKS

We stand as tall as angels

when we kneel to **help a friend.**

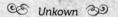 *Unkown*

*Negative labels placed on you when you were a
child can cripple your psyche well into adulthood.
Worse yet, the negative labels you place on others
can be even more devastating to you. Negative
labels are barriers or detours that can cut you off
from a kindred spirit. Then next time you venture
out into the world, try to leave your virtual stickers
and pen home and see what happens.*

გე

"**N**ext year we are going to be the kings of Forest
Park Elementary School!" Tom proclaimed to the
group of boys around us. "Sixth graders run this
place and things are going to be so different."

"Can anyone do a headstand?" Mike piped in. "I leaned against
my bedroom wall and did it last night."

My friend Jeff leaned over and asked me, "What are you doing during the Easter break? Wanna come over to my house
tomorrow?"

Before I could answer, the all-too-familiar rusted black car
pulled into the school parking lot.

"Run! It's Herman Munster!" Mike exclaimed as he darted
toward the school. The others in our group followed suit,
including me.

As I ran shrieking, I glanced over my shoulder to watch the
school's custodian emerge from his obsidian metal jalopy. *Herman Munster*, as the kids labeled him, was a tall, lanky, dark haired
man who was always dressed in a gray jumpsuit anchored by

husky, scuffed black boots. One boot had a thick extended heel and a metal brace to help him compensate for his deformed leg. This affliction caused him to walk with a slight limp, which only added to his Frankenstein-esque persona. Emotionless, he stood at the curb and watched us run from him pointing and screaming. Slowly, he trudged over to the side of the school, clamped onto the door handle of the gray vault door marked *Utility Room*, and disappeared into his stone-fortified dungeon.

"That's it everyone. Back inside. Recess is over!" the teacher exclaimed. "Head to the art room. Mrs. Kowalski is waiting for you."

"Great!" I thought as I made my way to the art room. "Art is one of my favorite classes! I can't wait to see what we are making today."

"Hello children," the art teacher said. "For Easter, we are all going to make angels to string up and down our hallways. Please take one of each of the blue and silver materials on the back table and return to your seats."

"Angels?" I muttered. "Why do we have to make Angels? That's for girls."

With an evil smirk I poked the boy next to me and whispered, "Watch this. I am going to make a devil. Do you know where the red and black paper is?" He pointed to the flat files. I went over to them and gathered my underworld essentials.

As I fashioned my little devil, the art teacher leaned over me and asked, "Do you really think *you* should be making *that* Mr. Clancy?"

"Well, you can't have angels without devils, can you Mrs. K?" I disrespectfully replied while the other children snickered.

With that, my red pitchfork-toting masterpiece was complete. I strung it into the long line of shimmering angels and watched it rise to take its foreboding position in the hallway

The end-of-day bell suddenly rang out and school was over for the next week. "Yay!" I exclaimed as I grabbed by book bag and headed for the bus. "Easter vacation!"

That night just after dinner, I decided to try to do a headstand following the instructions Mike revealed on the playground. Slowly I slid my feet up the wall. Almost there and, SMACK!

For a minute, I was dazed from the shock and thought my brother had hit me. As my head cleared, I felt a warm trickle run down my chin.

The three-pound ceramic Virgin Mary statue that used to be mounted on my bedroom wall was now lying next to my head. Her smile was almost mocking me as I touched my chin to subdue the now gushing scarlet flow. I was so embarrassed at my folly that I quickly bandaged up the one-inch gash on my chin and never said a word to my parents about the incident.

Thoughts of my little devil started racing through my head. "Did God just punish me?" I wondered. "I need to replace that devil with an angel or I am doomed!"

Hastily, I assembled the best angel I could with household materials. Once complete, I ran to the school with the angel in my hands. It was late and I was surprised that a car was still there. Unfortunately, its ominous profile meant there was only one person who could help me—*Herman Munster*. He was my only hope.

I knocked repeatedly on the glass door to the main hallway

with no response. Tears welled up in my eyes as I spied the tiny red demon dangling at the other end of the corridor. "Please come, Mr. Munster. I can't leave that thing in there for a week." Discouraged and saddened, I huddled up next to the door sobbing while I continued to knock in vain.

Suddenly, the broom bearing, gray-clad, monolith started down the hallway toward me. He sifted through a wad of keys and unlocked the door. Puzzled, he asked "What can I do for you, young man? Why so sad? Are you hurt?"

This was the first time I heard him speak and his gentle demeanor took me off guard. I went on to explain my irrational situation.

He chuckled and said, "I think we can fix that. Come show me where that little bad guy is and we'll take care of it."

He hoisted me up to the figurine. I swapped out the offending party and tossed it into a nearby garbage bin. After he set me down, I looked up at him and instead of saying 'thank you,' I said, "I'm sorry for calling you names and making fun of you."

He cracked a huge smile and said, "The name is Jim." He then pointed at his bad leg and said, "Polio. Got it when I was just a little guy. Had it all my life. I know it scares you kids, but I don't mind."

After a brief silence, he said, "You know, I've got one of the best jobs in the world. I get to see all of your little angel faces every day. I think about all of your smiles when I am sweeping the halls, and I go home blessed every night."

The following week, after Easter vacation, I stood at the edge of the playground wearing a huge smile waving hello to *Jim* as he stepped out of his car.

"Yep," I thought, "Tom was right. Things will definitely be different next year!"

In fact, they were different for the rest of my life.

Halos and Pitchforks

DEBT

It's good to

have money and the things that money can buy,
but it's good, too,
to check up once in a while and
make sure you haven't lost the
things that money can't buy.

George Horace Lorimer

You may build all of the wealth in the world, but if you are not building yourself the wealth is meaningless. How often do we see a news report on a celebrity who implodes? They seem to have everything going for themselves, yet they end up in a drug rehabilitation center or worse, dead. Build yourself through random acts of kindness and by extending a helping hand to those in need. Your compassion for others is a conduit for your success.

⁊

"That's a lot of money they owe us and they are over forty-five days late," my anxious partner said. "Do you think they are going to stiff us completely?" she questioned as she displayed our stack of mounting bills. "I need to pay these now or this could put our company under." The concern in her voice was at its highest level, and I knew our situation was critical.

"I called them this morning and they said they will have a check ready for us today," I replied in an attempt to calm her down. "I am going over to personally pick it up at one o'clock. We will be alright."

"I hope so," she shot back. "We need that check deposited and cleared as soon as possible."

"Better get my best suit jacket and tie on," I thought. "I need to look every part of the professional bill collector."

Skipping lunch, I jumped into my car and headed downtown. The delinquent client's office was located on the major thoroughfare of the city and parking would be tough. I ended up a few blocks away and hoofed it up to their office.

Once there, the receptionist greeted me.

"I am here to meet with the president," I announced. "He's expecting me."

"Sure thing," she replied. "Can I get you some coffee or water while you wait?"

"No thank you," I said, thinking about my next plan of attack to get that check and get it cashed fast. "I have only a short amount of time for this meeting. I shouldn't be here that long."

After a few minute wait, a voice echoed from the president's office. "Come on in!" he said.

We shook hands and smiled.

"Sorry for the delay in our payment. I really appreciate your patience," he said as he signed the check and handed it to me. "We are moving our offices out-of-state, and this created a lot of upheaval in our operations."

This was the largest single payment I had ever received. My mind swam in the richness I held in my hands. "Look at the length of that number," I thought as I slipped the check into my jacket pocket. "Not only is my company saved, but we can also expand!"

I shook his hand again and simply said, "Thanks, and uh… good luck with your move."

"Did you already have lunch?" he asked as I started for the door. "My treat."

"Thank you, but I am all set," I said with my sights firmly locked on getting to the bank. "I have other business I need to attend to and really need to get going."

I quickly left their office and was walking on air as I strolled down the sidewalk patting my right jacket pocket where my bankroll was stored. As I thought about all that money I barely noticed the army-fatigue-clad, homeless man following me and extending a handshake at me. I completely ignored his existence for an entire half block as I relished in my greed.

Instinctively, I shook his hand and was immediately pulled into a tight bear hug with both of my arms pinned to my side.

"Stop!" I exclaimed. "What are you doing? Hold on! Hold on!"

He tightened his grip further like a boa constrictor, while I basked in the idiocy of my words. "Well, that was a stupid thing to say," I scolded. "Just a minute," I blurted out as air left my lungs under the pressure of his embrace.

My cheeks turned rosy red as the embarrassment of my situation consumed me. "Can somebody please help me?" I pleaded to the passing business people, but I didn't even get a glance in return. It was as if I was sucked into a black hole of anonymity. "I am now as homeless as the guy attached to me," I thought. "Worthlessness is not a very good feeling."

Collapsing in submission after several failed attempts at escaping, I said to the homeless man, "I know you exist and you are not worthless. Successful people need to never lose sight that all people matter, no matter what their circumstances are. We must all care for and acknowledge each other. I am guilty of failing you in this regard, and I am truly sorry."

His grip loosened a bit as I compassionately said, "I need to see your eyes. I need to look into them to show you that what I am saying is genuine."

With that, he released me. As he stood with his gentle blue eyes locked on mine, he asked "How did you know? How did you know this was in my heart? How did you know?"

I solemnly shook my head and replied, "Isn't that what we should all be doing for each other? Money and success are worthless unless your heart is filled with compassion."

Suddenly a car horn blared behind me. I spun around to see what the commotion was. When I turned back around the homeless man had vanished. Baffled, I thought, "Where did he go? Was this one of those angel experiences or something?"

I continued down the street, this time patting my left jacket pocket, where true gold is stored.

Wall-Walkers

You cannot transcend

what you do not know. To go beyond yourself,

you must know yourself.

Sri Nisargadatta Maharaj

Be yourself and be true to yourself.
Only you and God know who you are. It's up
to you to show your true self to others. Do this
through your acts of kindness and caring.

꩜

"**L**et's head to the old school playground and do some jumps off the curb there," my friend Mike said as he mounted his BMX bike.

"Cool!" Tony replied as he slid his back tire out to kick up some dust.

"Let's cut through the woods at the end of the street. We can get in the schoolyard by the back gate near the field," I yelled. "Afterwards, we can head over to Dan's house and check out his new guitar and amp. I heard he's got a black, B.C. Rich Warlock and a 50 watt Marshall amp now."

"Cool! Sounds good!" the crew replied.

The conversation continued as we pedaled.

"Can you believe Randy Rhodes is gone?" I asked with a tone of depression. "He is one of the greatest guitarists ever. Why did he have to get in that plane?"

"Yeah, that totally sucks. I really wanted to see him in concert. Now I will never get the chance," Pat replied.

Everyone pursed their lips and shook their heads in agreement.

"Did you learn the guitar solo for *Over the Mountain* yet?" Mike inquired as we made our way feverishly along the edge of the road.

"No, I am still working on *Crazy Train* and a couple of solos off of Iron Maiden's *Number of the Beast* album," I replied, name dropping to add to my fame and glory.

"Battle of the bands, dude!" Mike exclaimed as he air-drummed on his handlebars. "My band has its sets down and we are ready to kick some ass!"

"We're getting there," I fired back. "Just got to keep practicing our sets. No doubt one of our groups is sure to take first place."

Mike just smirked and nodded his head.

"Did you see the poster in school with all of our bands listed?" Mike continued. "We are like rock stars at Colonie High! I can barely get down the hallway without people high-fiving me."

"It's good to be part of the in-crowd," I thought. "No worries here. I was finally cool."

As we reached the school grounds, our group skidded to an abrupt halt.

"What the heck it that?" Mike yelled, pointing his finger at the shocking sight.

"I think that's a punk rocker or something," Tony exclaimed as he started laughing. "Is Halloween early this year?"

The woman had lime-green, Mohawk-style hair, dark wrap-around sunglasses accentuated by heavy bright makeup, a spiked dog collar, a nose ring, knee-high black leather boots, and a pink tutu to cap off her look.

We stood motionless and bug-eyed on our bikes, gawking at

the spectacle. Just then, Mike jeered, "What a circus freak."

"Who dresses like that?" I questioned in disgust.

Hearing us, the woman waved and yelled, "Is that you, Bob?"

"Whaaaaa.....," I said as I trailed off in dismay. "She didn't just say my name, did she?"

"You know her?" Tony questioned in disbelief.

"No way!" I stammered. "I've never seen that freak in my life! Are you kidding me?"

"How does she know you then?" Tony teased. "Maybe you're secret lovers or something."

"Do you think I could keep something like *that* a secret?" I doled as proof of my innocence.

"Well, she sure knows you, doesn't she?" Mike rebutted. "I didn't know you were a closet punk-rocker."

As the woman walked closer to us, my mind raced. Finally, she stood directly in front of us.

"That is you. I know you. You are Bob Clancy," she said. I tried to scour my mind to make some sense of her words. "In fact, I know all of you. You two are Mike and Tony, right? And I think your name is Pat," she quizzed as she aimed her finger at each of my baffled friends.

"I don't think I know you," I said. "I think I'd remember that... or...um...you."

She removed her sunglasses, leaned in and stared into my eyes, and announced, "It's me...Lisa. I sat behind you in Spanish class all last year."

My dumbfounded expression made it obvious that I was straining to remember her.

"Well, I didn't look like this," she said chuckling. "Hmmmm...I didn't think you ever noticed me. Don't worry about it though. No one else ever acknowledged my existence either. I was a *wall-walker*—you know, those people who creep down the halls clinging to the lockers. The ones who don't matter. The kids no one cares about. The non-existent ones. Well, I am not invisible anymore, am I?"

For a moment I was taken aback by her eloquent demeanor. I humbly said, "You know, you've got a lot to say. You're actually pretty cool. It really takes guts to change yourself as much as you did. I am so sorry I never spoke to you before."

"Oh, it's okay. I am fine with who I am *now*," she responded. "I get to live a dream I never had the chance to in high school. You are lucky. You still have one more year left. Make the best of it and save a *wall-walker* for me. All you have to do is say 'hi' to them once in a while."

As I rode home alone that evening, I stopped on a hill and gazed down my empty street to reflect. "I've been a part of degrading her life by simply ignoring her," I thought. "Was I too busy trying to be someone I thought everyone else wanted me to be just to fit in? How many times did she sit there behind me hoping I would just say hello? What a powerful difference one small word can make in redeeming someone else's life."

Compassion

If you want
others to be happy,
practice compassion.
If you want to be happy,
practice compassion.

Dalai Lama

*a*n interviewer once asked famed anthropologist Dr. Margaret Mead about the earliest signs of civilization she looks for in a given culture. He expected the answer to be the discovery of a tool, craft, or art form. But Dr. Mead replied, "A healed femur."

Mead explained that no mended bones are found where *survival of the fittest* reigns. When someone breaks a femur, they can't survive to hunt, fish, or escape enemies unless they have help from someone else. A healed femur shows that someone cared. Someone had to do that injured person's hunting and gathering until their leg healed. "Compassion," Mead said, "is the first sign of civilization." [1]

Have you added compassion to your daily routine?
Here are some thoughts to consider:

ᕦ

"The whole idea of compassion is based on a keen awareness
of the interdependence of all these living beings, which are
all part of one another, and all involved in one another."
Thomas Merton

"A love for humanity came over me, and watered and fertilized
the fields of my inner world which had been lying fallow, and
this love of humanity vented itself in a vast compassion."
Georg Brandes

---

1. E. K. Rowell, 1001 Quotes, Illustrations & Humourous Stories. Baker Books, 2006., p. 210.

"Computers are magnificent tools for the realization of our dreams, but no machine can replace the human spark of spirit, compassion, love, and understanding."
Louis Gerstner

"Compassion, in which all ethics must take root, can only attain its full breadth and depth if it embraces all living creatures and does not limit itself to mankind."
Albert Schweitzer

"Happiness and peace will come to earth only as the light of love and human compassion enter the souls of men."
David O. McKay

HALL PASS

Room Number: _____

_____

Teacher: _____

Spaz

Never be

bullied into silence.
Never allow yourself
to be made a victim.
Accept no one's definition of your life;
define yourself.

Harvey Fierstein

*Everything that happens to you, good or bad, is
in some respect your own fault. Even so, you
should never blame yourself for the negative
things. When the odds are stacked against you
is the time when you need to grab the reins of
your life—because only you can change your fate.
Always take a moment to shine in the beauty of
yourself and what you are capable of.*

☙

"Spaz! Spaz! Spaz! Spaz!" echoed the taunting voices of my schoolmates in the locker lined hallway.

"Look at the dork!" one kid yelled as he pointed at the small shy boy toting his pancake-stacked, paper-stuffed binders. Often these taunts would make the boy erupt in a screaming fit that the inhospitable crowd would relish. Today, there was a special bonus in store for him and the unruly mob.

Fred, our school bully, smelled blood in the water and didn't hesitate to flex his dominance over the weak. "52 card pickup!" Fred yelled, and then WOOSH! The hallway instantly filled with a ticker tape parade of wrinkled papers, laughter, and the bloodcurdling shriek of the pint-sized blonde haired boy.

Propping his black, thick-rimmed glasses back onto his face, the boy wiped the drizzle from his nose with the back of his hand and began to collect his sheets.

Feeling pity for this poor kid, I grabbed as many of his papers as I could while others just left their shoe prints on them. As I handed my stack to him, Fred jeered, "Why are you helping this loser?"

With apathetic disdain, I replied, "No, Fred, the question is why *aren't* you helping him?"

My commentary was enough to get Fred to leave, but the damaged soul in front of me was far from repairable.

"God, I hate middle school!" I said trying to comfort him. "Don't let them get to you. You are smarter than them and that's why they pick on you." Attempting to lighten the mood, I then added, "Just so you know, when they were giving out brains, Fred thought they said trains so he didn't take one."

The boy didn't say a word. He just curved his lips enough for me to make out a modest smile. Before we parted, the boy slowly turned his head toward me. I detected a glint of hope in his eyes.

Almost two weeks to the day, the same ugly hallway scene unfolded. "Spaz! Spaz! Spaz! Spaz!" the mob lashed out. Pushing his way through the crowd, Fred exclaimed, "Looks like we're in for another paper snowstorm, compliments of Spaz!" But before Fred finished his sentence, the boy catapulted his paper-filled grenade into the air.

As the three-holed flack drifted down around him and Fred, I joyously observed the boy grinning from ear-to-ear with his hands high in the air. Like the wave at a sports arena, the crowd switched from taunting him to cheering him on like a hero in lower Manhattan parade.

That day, Spaz became a legend in our middle school, and he wore his label like a medal. It just goes to show that taking matters into your own hands to control your fate can often be a deciding factor in your destiny. Never underestimate how powerful you can be by conquering a negative label placed upon you.

ROAD RAGE

To win
one hundred victories
in one hundred battles
is not the highest skill.
**To subdue the enemy
without fighting
is the highest skill.**

Sun Tsu

There are always potholes and roadblocks on your life's highway. You can choose to crash into them and damage yourself, or you can carefully drive around them. There is always a silver lining in everything. You just have to take the time to recognize what that is. Be open to it.

❦

*I*t's a long, arduous, physically challenging and painful road to simultaneously earn a fourth degree master black belt in two different martial arts. In my own quest to achieve this lofty goal in Tae Kwon Do and Combat Hapkido, I've gained a very important sense. I feel the more you sharpen your defensive fighting skills, the less likely you will ever need to use them.

My many years of martial arts training has given me a cool, confident, clear-thinking attitude and a positive outlook on life. When faced with stressful or alarming situations, I am able to defuse myself in order to prevent things from escalating to the ugly. My recent experience proved this point.

"It looks like we're going to have to battle a little five o'clock traffic to get home," I said to my twelve-year-old son. "I think everybody just got out of work at the same time. At this rate, you will probably be thirteen by the time we get home."

"Yeah, right, Dad," he said as he lowered his iPod. "It's okay. I'm not in a hurry."

"Me neither," I responded as I relaxed back in my seat.

Glancing out of my rearview mirror, I saw at least a dozen cars racked up behind me. "Well, at least I'm the first one in line at this red light. We should hopefully have clear sailing home from here."

The light switched to green and I started driving through the intersection. Without warning, some guy, speeding like a maniac on the shoulder of the road, passed all of the cars in my lane.

I was the lead car in the column and I didn't see this idiot coming as he ripped past me kicking up dust and rocks. Startled, I honked my horn at him just as he missed clipping my passenger side fender.

"Did you see that?" I exclaimed.

"No, but I heard it coming. The car was right next to my window, Dad," my son replied as he dropped his iPod. "I'm really scared."

It was then that I realized this was intentional as I watched the jerk wave both of his hands in the air while his car swerved erratically. He slammed on his brakes and stopped his white, luxury sedan just short of the next red light. I pulled around him into the left passing lane so I wouldn't be trapped behind him if things took a turn for the worse—and they did.

Apparently, he must have viewed my maneuver as a threat. He jumped out of his car screaming, "Oh, so you want to be an asshole about it! You got somethin' to say?"

"Great. This guy is not in control of himself," I thought as my adrenaline started kicking up.

I rolled my window down and asked him, "What's wrong with you? Are you nuts? You're going to kill someone driving like that!"

He started another filth-ridden rant, so I did a loud, sharp ki-hap (a Tae Kwon Do verbal roar) and yelled, "Hey! Shut your foul mouth and get back into your car now!"

This stunned him for a minute and he slumped back into his driver's seat. Stewing about being put in his place, he suddenly sprang from his car again, this time with increased rage.

He stomped toward my car, postured himself like a gorilla in heat, pumped his fists, and yelled, "Let's go tough guy. Let's see what you can do. You wanna show off for your *punk kid*?"

This man was far from my typical kindred spirit, but in this moment, his words reminded me of what's important—my son and my job as role model for him.

I chuckled at him, shook my head, and calmly said, "Buddy, you don't even know what you are getting yourself into. You are really not worth anyone's time and certainly not mine or my son's. Oh, and thank you for putting on a show for all the witnesses here."

As he glanced to look at the pile of cars he was holding up with his antics, I pulled away slowly, smiled, waved my hand at him, and hollered, "Bye! Bye! You have a nice day!"

Standing alone in the middle of the intersection, his hands abruptly drooped to his side like wet noodles. They were a nice side dish to accompany his bruised ego. I am sure his audience thoroughly enjoyed that entrée.

It was the best way I could *show off* and be an example for my *punk kid*.

Road Rage

Two Hearts

If our hearts are in pain
and it becomes too much to bear,
Hold me. I'll hold you.
Know that I still care.

If our love wavers
and seasons start to change,
Hold me. I'll hold you.
We'll see the sun again.

When we are older
and our lives begin to fade,
Hold me. I'll hold you.
We'll be another day.

If a storm rages
and it separates our hearts,
Hold me. I'll hold you.
We'll make another start.

Once you see
our love will always be,
Hold me. I'll hold you,
drifting endlessly.

෧ *Robert Clancy* ෨

Stranded
GAS

The only time

you should look down at someone

is when you are helping them up.

Jesse Jackson

*It seems that one of the hardest things
for most people to do is lend a helping hand
to a stranger. Fear or some other stumbling block
prevents them from getting involved. If we all
make small efforts to reach out to each other,
the world will be better place for all of us.
Someday, you just might be that stranger
stranded on the side of the road.*

⟡

Several years ago my wife and I were on Interstate 87 heading south when we ran out of gas. We were somewhere between Glens Falls, NY and Saratoga Springs, NY, in the highway's "no man's land." The gas gauge on our car stopped working a week earlier, and I could only judge how much fuel remained by the miles traveled between fill ups. For some reason we ran out of fuel much sooner than expected.

As our car coasted to a dead stop on the shoulder of the highway, we both started to panic. The nearest gas station was miles away and there was no cell phone service where we were. I broke into a cold sweat thinking about the daunting walk I was going to have to get help.

"Oh no! Are we out of gas? What are we going to do now?" my wife nervously questioned.

"I am not sure. I will probably have to walk it. I don't think anyone will stop for us. How many times have we sailed past a stranded car on the road?"

"I know," she replied. "Do we have any water in here?" she questioned as she began to take inventory of our survival gear. "It's really hot out there today. Can you try to start the car again?"

I turned the key several more times before resigning to the fact that the car was not going anywhere. "We are dead in the water," I said. "It's going to be a very tough afternoon. I am going to pop the hood to check out the engine."

Before I got out of the car to open the engine compartment, I heard a faint voice emanating from behind us.

"Did you hear that?" my wife questioned in disbelief.

I quickly spun my head around and saw a red pickup truck parked directly behind us. "Where the heck did he come from?" I asked.

"I'm not sure," my wife said. "He just appeared out of no-where."

The man then yelled out again, "Do you need help? Did you run out of gas?"

Slightly embarrassed by our predicament, I sheepishly yelled back, "Yeah, it's bone dry."

Holding up a red gas can he said, "I am so lucky I found you!"

"Lucky *you* found *us*?" I questioned in puzzlement.

"I hope you don't think I am a crazy person or something," he replied as he walked up and shook my hand. "The name's Jim," he continued. "I was once stranded on the side of the highway just like you, and some kind soul stopped to help me. He was a lifesaver! After he drove me to a gas station and got me going, he just asked me to help someone else in need. I've been waiting to pay it forward for almost a year now! It's the best way I can honor him. After all, shouldn't we all be lending a hand to each other?"

"You know, you are right, Jim," I replied. "I've left many people stranded thinking someone else will stop for them. That someone should have been me."

The man drove us both to a service station, paid for our gas, bought us both a soda, and drove us back to our car. He even filled our tank like an old-time service attendant.

"That should do it," he said as he rubbed his hands together in approval. "Let's see if that will get you on your way."

As the car engine fired up, the man could all but drink in the relief that poured over our eyes.

"I can't thank you enough for this, Jim," I said in a humbled tone.

"No need to thank me. It's just your turn to pay it forward!" he said. "If you ever see someone in need of help, just stop and lend them a hand. Sometimes the thought that someone cares makes all the difference in the world."

"I will do this, Jim," I said with a smile. "I promise!"

After this encounter, I thought, "How many countless disabled cars and distressed people have I passed over? I've really got to make a change in myself. I need to keep this chain reaction going."

The next day, I purchased a five-gallon gas can and jumper cables and placed them in the back compartment of my car. I was prepared.

A few weeks later, while exiting a mall parking lot, I noticed a distressed woman standing next to a car with its hood up. I doubled back and pulled my car in across from hers. I quickly jumped out, grabbed my jumper cables, and asked, "Do you need help?"

She looked up at me somewhat startled and said, "Yes! Yes! Yes! You are an angel."

With tears streaming down her cheeks she continued, "I must have asked over thirty people for help and they either ignored me or were too busy to help. I just gave up when you appeared from nowhere with jumper cables."

As I hooked up the cables to her battery, I told her the story about the man who helped my wife and me earlier that month. She smiled and said, "There really are angels out there watching over us, aren't there?"

"Yes," I said confidently. "Thank you for allowing me to be your angel for today."

With a cheerful glow in her eye, she hugged me and asked, "How can I repay you for this?"

I simply smiled and said, "No need to repay or thank me; just pay it forward."

Final Thoughts

A smile is a light
in the window of the soul
indicating that the heart is home.

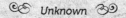 Unknown

Creativity

Why start thinking out of the box when you can start by thinking without the box! Take a fresh look at everything in as many different ways as you can.

Service

Do something good with your life and do it for something greater than yourself!

Leadership

Be a leader not a follower, and realize that sometimes you need to lead by following. Handle difficult choices with grace and be accountable for your mistakes.

Mistakes

If you have to do something again, do it better the second time through. A mistake is the best way to find a better solution.

Success

Be a *how* thinker, not a *what if* thinker. Anything is possible to achieve as long as you have the following at hand—time, resources, and creative solutions. All ideas should always be kept on the table.

Challenges

Life will always provide you with challenges, but you should never see barriers. Barriers are just temporary obstructions that get tunneled through, driven around, climbed over, or simply blown up.

Aging

Take time to enjoy the little things in life and you will age like fine wine.

Smiles

A smile might get you the job you just interviewed for, it might help you land that contract you've been vying for, and it will most certainly make someone else's life a bit brighter.

Judgment

Although people don't get a second chance to make a first impression, hold your labels and just enjoy the process of getting to know one another.

Labels

Shed that negative label someone placed on you or put a positive spin on it. It matters most what *you* think about *yourself*.

☙

Just as Dr. Albert Schweitzer asked Hugh O'Brian, "What are you going to do with this?" I am going to pose this same challenge to you. Take this time to reflect on the kindred spirits who have shaped and guided your life. Think deeply about the time you've volunteered to help someone in need. Smile a bit more, share a hug, and tell others about your wonderful experiences. Continue to make a difference in the world, and always know that you already have just by being you.

If you've written a compelling story on a kindred spirit, a lesson in compassion, or a captivating view on volunteerism, I would love to read it! To have your story considered for the follow-up book *The Hitchhiker's Guide to the Soul: In the Shoes of Others*, stay connected and learn more at www.guidetothesoul.com.

Supporting Others

> "Ideals are like stars: you will not succeed in
> touching them with your hands, but like the seafaring
> man on the desert of waters, you choose them as your guides,
> and following them you reach your destiny."
> *Carl Schurz*

The author has selected a portion of the proceeds from the sale of this book to benefit the New York East Hugh O'Brian Youth Leadership Seminar, which fosters youth leadership through community service and Junior Achievement of Northeastern New York, an organization that inspires and prepares young people for work readiness, entrepreneurship, and financial literacy through the use of experiential, hands-on programs.

Inspiring, Educational, Compassionate, Energizing, Enthusiastic, Motivating, Transforming, Long-Lasting, and Life-Changing

These are some of the words that students, schools, parents, alumni, volunteers, and supporters use to describe Hugh O'Brian Youth Leadership (HOBY).

Founded in 1958, HOBY's mission is to inspire and develop our global community of youth and volunteers to a life dedicated to leadership, service, and innovation. HOBY programs are conducted annually throughout the United States, serving local and international high school students.

The New York East Leadership Seminar provides youth in eastern New York a unique three-day motivational leadership training, service learning, and motivation-building experience. New York East HOBY also provides adults with opportunities to make a significant impact on the lives of youth by volunteering.

NYE Hugh O'Brian Youth Leadership Seminar
PO Box 14471, Albany, NY 12212-4471
www.hobynye.org

oℓ

Explore the Power of JA

Junior Achievement is Northeastern New York's largest organization dedicated to educating students about issues relating to work readiness, entrepreneurship, and financial literacy through the use of experiential, hands-on programs. In partnership with the business and education communities, and through the support of community volunteers, JA brings the real world to students, opening their minds to their potential.

Junior Achievement of Northeastern New York, Inc.
8 Stanley Circle, Latham, NY 12110
phone: (518) 783-4336
www.janeny.org

About the Author

Robert Clancy is an entrepreneur, professional speaker, and author living in the heart of Tech Valley in upstate New York. He is co-founder and Managing Partner of Spiral Design Studio, one of the largest full-service graphic design and web development firms in the Northeast. Spiral Design specializes in taking corporate brands, marketing campaigns, and digital media from ordinary to extraordinary. Spiral Design Studio's clients have included dozens of corporations, educational & healthcare organizations, non-profits and startups, including Citicorp, Home Depot, Sears, Activision, Disney, Albany Medical Center, University at Albany, The NYS Dental Association, and Junior Achievement of Northeastern NY, among many others.

As early as age six, Robert had immense compassion for humanity. He commits his life to assisting others, whether volunteering, helping them to succeed, or even just offering a friendly smile. Robert is a husband, father, and 4th Degree Master Black Belt Instructor of Tae Kwon Do. Through many years of volunteer work, he's amassed a collection of awards and has served in leadership positions for Hugh O'Brian Youth Leadership (HOBY), Junior Achievement, the American Marketing Association, and the Graphic Artists Guild, among others.

Robert Clancy is a dedicated volunteer who completely embodies the spirit of service—a selfless commitment to helping others make a positive difference in the world.

Spiral Design Studio, LLC
135 Mohawk Street
Cohoes NY 12047
ph: (518) 326-1135 • fx: (518) 326-2342
www.spiraldesign.com

More Hitchhiker's Guide to the Soul!

Do you have a compelling story about a kindred spirit, a lesson in compassion, or a captivating view on volunteerism that has changed your life? If so, I invite you to submit your story to be considered for publication in the upcoming follow up book *The Hitchhiker's Guide to the Soul: In the Shoes of Others.*

Stories may be up to fifteen hundred words and must be either a lesson in compassion or a captivating story on volunteerism that is uplifting and inspiring. You may submit your own original piece, something you've read, or your favorite inspirational quote.

To obtain a copy of the submission guidelines and submit your story, please visit the Hitchhiker's Guide to the Soul website at www.guidetothesoul.com or contact us at the address below.

We ensure that all original submissions are credited.

For submissions, guidelines, and more information:

The Hitchhiker's Guide to the Soul Submissions
c/o: Spiral Design Studio
135 Mohawk Street
Cohoes, NY 12047
Phone: (518) 326-1135
Fax: (518) 326-2342

email: submissions@guidetothesoul.com
www.guidetothesoul.com

Speaking Opportunities

Have the author speak at your next event! Robert Clancy's compelling speaking engagements and learning seminars are now available for your company, charity, or volunteer organization! In his signature keynote speech, *Scenic Views of Volunteerism: From Kindred Spirits to Lessons in Compassion,* Robert uses examples from his book, *The Hitchhiker's Guide to the Soul*, to illustrate how volunteerism and a compassion for humanity can help shape the future.

For all inquiries please contact us at:

The Hitchhiker's Guide to the Soul
c/o: Spiral Design Studio
135 Mohawk Street
Cohoes, NY 12047
Phone: (518) 326-1135
Fax: (518) 326-2342

email: inquiries@guidetothesoul.com
www.guidetothesoul.com

15601893R00115

Made in the USA
Charleston, SC
11 November 2012